Dziadzia Gienek's Authentic Polish Desserts

91 Easy Recipes for Delicious Cakes, Cookies, and Treats That Make You Nostalgic for Warm Family Gatherings

Copyright © 2025 by HarvestGuard Publications – All rights reserved.

No portion of this book may be reproduced in any form without written permission from the publisher or author, except as permitted by U.S. copyright law.

This publication is designed to provide accurate and authoritative information in regard to the subject matter covered. It is sold with the understanding that neither the author nor the publisher is engaged in rendering legal, investment, accounting or other professional services. While the publisher and author have used their best efforts in preparing this book, they make no representations or warranties with respect to the accuracy or completeness of the contents of this book and specifically disclaim any implied warranties of merchantability or fitness for a particular purpose. No warranty may be created or extended by sales representatives or written sales materials. The advice and strategies contained herein may not be suitable for your situation. You should consult with a professional when appropriate. Neither the publisher nor the author shall be liable for any loss of profit or any other commercial damages, including but not limited to special, incidental, consequential, personal, or other damages.

Dziadzia Gienek spent 60 years creating each dessert with passion & commitment!

FROM OUR FAMILY TO YOURS!

Table of Contents

Introduction — VI

1. Cakes & Tortes — 1
   (Ciasta i Torty)
2. Cookies & Small Sweets — 29
   (Ciastka i Słodycze)
3. Pastries & Breads — 49
   (Wypieki i Pieczywo)
4. Other Traditional Polish Desserts — 71
5. Conclusion — 97

Glossary — 101
   Cakes & Tortes (Ciasta i Torty)
   Cookies & Small Sweets (Ciastka i Słodycze)
   Pastries & Breads (Wypieki i Pieczywo)
   Other Traditional Polish Desserts

Introduction

There's a kind of magic that lives in the kitchen—a magic passed down through flour-dusted aprons, the scent of warm cinnamon drifting through the air, and the quiet joy of seeing a loved one's eyes light up at the first bite of something familiar. For our family, that magic came from **Dziadzia Gienek**, my beloved father, whose hands shaped not just dough but the very heart of our family traditions.

He wasn't a famous chef. He didn't own a bakery or had gone to a renowned pastry college in Paris. What he had was something even more valuable: a deep, intuitive understanding of flavor, family, and the kind of love that could be tasted in every bite of his desserts.

Whether it was his buttery sernik (Polish cheesecake) brought out during Easter, his flaky faworki (angel wings) during Easter, or his rich makowiec (poppy seed roll) during Christmas, Dziadzia Gienek's sweets were always more than just food—they were invitations. Invitations to sit down, slow down, and savor life together.

That's what this book is about.

The Heartbeat of a Polish Kitchen

In Polish culture, food isn't just nourishment—it's a conversation, a memory, a celebration. And desserts? They're the soul of it all. Every celebration, from weddings to name days to Sunday suppers, ends with something sweet. But more than that, dessert is often the quiet reward after a long day, the comfort after a storm, the thing we gather around even when there's nothing to celebrate.

For generations, Polish families have passed down dessert recipes like heirlooms. Carefully measured by hand, scribbled in the margins of old notebooks, or simply memorized through repetition, these recipes tell the story of a people who have always found beauty in simplicity.

And in our family, those stories always began with dziadzia Gienek.

He was born in a small town nestled between rolling hills and thick forests, where seasons ruled the rhythm of life and every ingredient came with a story. He learned to bake from his own mother—my grandmother—who believed that sugar was best used with a light hand and that every cake was an act of patience.

After immigrating to the West, Gienek brought these recipes with him. He didn't have much when he arrived, but what he did have was an incredible ability to make people feel welcome—and a plate of his ciasto drożdżowe (yeast cake) could do just that.

More Than Just Recipes

This book is not just a collection of 91 dessert recipes—it's a tribute. A tribute to the old wooden table in Dziadzia's kitchen, where the smell of apple szarlotka baking in the oven could turn an ordinary Tuesday into something special. It's a celebration of the quiet rituals—sifting flour together, licking the spoon, sneaking a warm cookie when no one's looking—that brought our family close.

Each recipe you'll find in these pages has been tested, refined, and lovingly translated for the modern kitchen. They're not overly complicated or fussy because Gienek didn't believe in making things harder than they needed to be. He believed in making things *delicious* and always with heart.

In fact, many of the recipes were once little scribbles on the back of grocery lists or tucked into the pages of a well-worn cookbook. Over time, I compiled them, tested them, and adapted them slightly where needed—ensuring they were accessible for today's home cooks without losing the spirit of the originals.

You don't need to be an expert baker to use this book. All you need is a love for tradition, a bit of curiosity, and the willingness to get your hands a little sticky with dough.

A Taste of Nostalgia

We live in a fast world, one where meals are often rushed and convenience overshadows craftsmanship. But baking, especially the kind that comes from old-world traditions, invites us to slow down. To pay attention. To connect.

There's something incredibly grounding about kneading dough by hand or watching yeast rise. It's in these small, quiet moments that we're reminded of those who came before us—of the kitchens where we first fell in love with the smell of warm vanilla or the sound of a bubbling jam filling a tart crust.

For many of us, Polish desserts are tied to our deepest memories. The soft crumble of a honey cake at our grandparent's house. The powdered sugar dust on our noses after biting into pączki. The hours spent making piernik during the holidays, the smell of cloves and ginger wrapping around us like a wool blanket.

Even if you didn't grow up with these flavors, I promise you this: they have a way of making you *feel* at home.

What You'll Find Inside

This book is organized to make your dessert journey as easy—and fun—as possible. Whether you're baking for a special occasion or just want something sweet with your coffee, you'll find something that fits. Here's a quick taste of what's ahead:

- **Cakes & Loaves**: From light and airy babkas to dense, moist honey cakes, these are the showstoppers of any Polish gathering.
- **Cookies & Bites**: Think jam-filled kolaczki, vanilla kipferl, and nutty crescents—perfect for gifting or snacking.
- **Pączki & Fritters**: Yes, the beloved Polish donuts get their moment here, along with a few crispy carnival favorites.
- **Holiday Favorites**: Desserts made just for Christmas, Easter, and other special moments, all rich in tradition.
- **Everyday Treats**: Simple, comforting recipes that bring joy to even the most ordinary day.

Each recipe includes easy-to-follow instructions, helpful tips, and a little story or memory when available—because every dessert has its place in the larger picture of family and faith.

Why Polish Desserts?

Polish desserts have a unique balance of richness and restraint. They're flavorful but not overpowering, sweet but not cloying, and they reflect a history of resilience, resourcefulness, and deep-rooted joy.

In Poland, baking has always been about making the most of what's available—turning modest ingredients into something extraordinary. A few eggs, some flour, a bit of butter and sugar… and suddenly, you have a centerpiece for Sunday dinner. A reason to gather. A reason to smile.

That's what Dziadzia Gienek taught me - that food is never *just* food. It's the language of love, the glue of generations, and the shared thread that ties our past to our present.

A Personal Invitation

As you turn these pages and begin your own baking journey, I hope you'll feel the warmth of Dziadzia's kitchen—the laughter, the music, the clatter of mixing bowls, and the hush that falls over the room when the first slice is served.

I hope you make these recipes your own, adding your own flair and creating your own memories along the way. Above all, I hope you share them with your family, your friends, and those who might need a little taste of comfort in their lives.

Because that's what Gienek would have wanted. Not just to preserve tradition but to keep it alive through joy, through food, and through togetherness.

So grab your apron. Preheat your oven. And welcome to the heart of our family.

Let's bake something beautiful together.

Chapter One

Cakes & Tortes
(Ciasta i Torty)

Sernik

Polish Cheesecake

| SERVES: 4-6 SLICES | PREP TIME: 40 MIN | BAKING TIME: 45 MIN | CHILLING TIME: 3-4 HOURS |

In Poland, Sernik is so cherished that nearly every family claims their own special recipe as the "best." Family members often humorously compete to see whose cheesecake receives the most compliments during festive gatherings!

Ingredients

Crust
- **200g (7 oz)** digestive biscuits or graham crackers (traditional Polish alternative: shortcrust pastry).
- **100 g (7 tbsp)** unsalted butter, melted

Cheesecake Filling
- **1 kg (2.2 lbs)** Polish farmer's cheese (twaróg) *(or ricotta/cottage cheese blended smooth)*
- **200 g (1 cup)** granulated sugar
- **5** large eggs
- **100 g (7 tbsp)** unsalted butter, melted and cooled
- **200 ml (¾ cup)** sour cream or heavy cream
- **2 tbsp** potato starch or cornstarch
- **1 tsp** vanilla extract
- **Zest of 1** lemon *(optional, for extra flavor)*

Optional Topping
- Powdered sugar *(traditional)*
- Chocolate glaze or fresh fruits

Instructions

Prepare the Crust
- Preheat oven to **175°C (350°F)**.
- Crush biscuits into fine crumbs. Combine with melted butter until evenly moistened.
- Press the mixture firmly into the bottom of a **9-inch (23 cm)** springform pan.
- Bake crust for **10 minutes**. Remove and allow to cool.

Prepare the Cheesecake Filling
- In a large mixing bowl, blend twaróg (or substitute cheese) until smooth and creamy.
- Beat eggs and sugar separately until pale and fluffy, then add to the cheese mixture.
- Stir in melted butter, sour cream, vanilla extract, lemon zest, and potato starch. Mix thoroughly until smooth.

Bake the Sernik
- Pour the filling onto the crust and smooth the surface.
- Bake at **175°C (350°F) for 60–70 minutes**, until the edges are set but the center still slightly jiggles.
- Turn off the oven, crack open the oven door, and leave the cheesecake inside for 30 minutes to cool gradually *(this prevents cracking)*.
- Remove and allow to cool completely at room temperature.

Chill and Serve
- Refrigerate the cheesecake for at least 4 hours (overnight is best) to achieve a perfect texture.
- Dust generously with powdered sugar, or add toppings like fresh fruit or chocolate glaze if desired.
- Slice and serve chilled or at room temperature.

Storage Tips
- Store cheesecake in an airtight container in the refrigerator for 4–5 days.
- Cheesecake tastes best prepared the day before serving, allowing flavors to develop fully.
- Sernik can be frozen for up to 3 months when rapped securely.

Ciocia Wiesia's Sernik

Aunt Wiesia's *Cheesecake*

SERVES: 6-8 SLICES	PREP TIME: 20 MIN	BAKING TIME: 40-45 MIN	CHILLING TIME: 1 HOUR

This Sernik recipe is our family's secret recipe. Every Polish family has their own secret cheesecake; this one is ours. If you make it, you will love it and everyone will want you to share the recipe. If they do, please ask them to buy this book! 🤗 This way they can have them all! From our family to yours. Enjoy!

Ingredients

Cheesecake Filling
- **1 pack** of cream cheese (Elite Lite)
- **8 Egg yolks** (Keep the whites in a separate bowl)
- **2 tablespoons** of softened butter
- **1 cup** white sugar
- **1 teaspoon** of vanilla sugar or extract
- **1 tablespoon** semolina
- **1 tablespoon** potato or corn flour

Note: Beat it on low to mix all ingredients in a bowl until well incorporated and smooth.

Sour Cream Icing
- **3/4 cup** of 14% sour cream (For a thicker layer, use 250 ml of sour cream)
- **1 teaspoon** of vanilla sugar (If unavailable, replace it with 1 teaspoon of vanilla extract)
- **4-5 tablespoons** of white sugar

Note: Beat it on low until the sugar melts and the mixture becomes soft and easy to spread on the cheesecake.

Instructions

Prepare the Cheesecake Filling

Egg Yolk Part
- Preheat oven to **177°C (350°F).**
- Beat the **egg yolk with 1/2 of the sugar** in a bowl. Once the sugar is completely incorporated, add the cream cheese. Once incorporated, add the flour. Then, add the **vanilla extract** or vanilla sugar and beat it on low until all is incorporated and smooth. At the very end you fold in the melted butter and beat until fully incorporated.

Egg White Part
- Mix egg whites on high until they become set and stiff. Add the rest of the sugar and mix on medium until the sugar is fully incorporated.

Combine The Two Parts
- Fold the egg whites part into the egg yolk part and mix delicately with a spoon until fully combined.

Bake the Sernik
- Pour the filling into a medium-sized baking dish lined with parchment paper. The cheesecake filling should be 2 inches thick for best results. Smooth it with a spatula.
- Bake at **177°C (350°F) for 20-25 minutes**, then lower the oven temperature to **160°C (320°F) for 30 minutes** until **golden** brown.
- Add a **tray filled with warm water** and place it on the bottom rack to prevent the cheesecake from cracking.
- Once baked and ready, turn the oven off, remove the cheesecake halfway on the rack, pour the icing on top, and spread it evenly.
- Put it back in the oven for 10 minutes. The icing will set. Take it out and let it rest.

Chill and Serve
- Let the cheesecake rest at room temperature for **1 hour** to achieve a perfect texture.
- Slice and serve at room temperature.

Storage Tips
- Store cheesecake in an airtight container in the refrigerator for 4-5 days.
- Sernik can be frozen for up to 3 months when rapped securely.

Makowiec
Polish Poppy Seed Roll

SERVES: 12 SLICES **PREP TIME: 30 MIN** **RESTING TIME: 1.5 HOURS** **BAKING TIME: 30-40 MINS**

In Poland, Makowiec is believed to bring luck, prosperity, and abundance. In some regions of Poland, it was even believed that eating poppy seeds would help you see dreams of the future.

Ingredients

For the Dough
- **500g (4 cups)** all-purpose flour
- **7g (2¼ tsp)** dry yeast or **25g** fresh yeast
- **100g (½ cup)** granulated sugar
- **200ml (¾ cup)** warm milk
- **2 large** eggs
- **100g (7 tbsp)** unsalted butter, melted
- **½ tsp** salt
- **1 tsp** vanilla extract

Poppy Seed Filling
- **250g (1½ cups)** ground poppy seeds
- **150ml (½ cup)** hot milk
- **100g (½ cup)** granulated sugar
- **2 tbsp** honey
- **50g (⅓ cup)** raisins (optional)
- **50g (⅓ cup)** chopped walnuts or almonds (optional)
- **1** egg white (beaten)
- **½ tsp** almond extract (optional)
- **1 tsp** lemon zest

Optional Topping
- Powdered sugar *(traditional)*
- Lemon juice

Instructions

Prepare the Crust
- In a small bowl, dissolve the yeast in warm milk with 1 tbsp of sugar. Let sit for 10 mins.
- In a large mixing bowl, combine flour, sugar, and salt.
- Add eggs, melted butter, vanilla extract, and yeast mixture. Mix well and knead for 10 minutes until the dough is elastic and smooth.
- Cover with kitchen towel and let rise for 1 to 1.5 hours or until double in size.

Prepare the Cheesecake Filling
- in a saucepan, and combine ground poppy seeds and hot milk. Stir and simmer for 5 minutes, then let cool.
- Add sugar, honey, raisins, chopped nuts, lemon zest, almond extract, and beaten egg whites. Mix.

Assemble the Rolls
- Preheat the oven to 180 degrees Celsius or 350 degrees Fahrenheit.
- Punch the dough and divide it into two equal parts.
- Roll out each piece into a rectangle (about 30x40cm or 12x16 inches).
- Spread half of the poppy seed filling evenly over each rectangle, leaving a small border on the edges.
- Roll the dough tightly into a log. Pinch edges to seal.
- Place the rolls seam-side down on a lined baking sheet.

Bake the Makowiec
- Brush the rolls with egg yolk and milk mixture. Let rest for 15 mins.
- Bake for 35 to 40 minutes, until golden brown.
- Glaze with powdered sugar or lemon juice and serve.

Storage Tips
- Makowiec can be safely stored in the refrigerator for up to a week.
- To freeze, slice each roll into pieces, carefully wrap each piece in plastic wrap, and place them in a freezer-safe bag or plastic container. Makowiec can be safely frozen for up to three months.

Karpatka
Polish Cream Puff Cake

SERVES: 12   **PREP TIME: 30 MINS**   **COOKING TIME: 1.5 HOURS**   **CHILLING TIME: 2+ HOURS**

Karpatka gets its name from the Carpathian Mountains (Karpaty) because its puffy, uneven choux pastry layers resemble rugged mountain peaks. Its creamy vanilla filling makes it a beloved homemade treat across Poland.

Ingredients

For the Choux Pastry (Ciastro Parzone)
- **250 ml (1 cup)** water
- **125g (1/2 cup)** unsalted butter
- **4** large eggs
- **1/2 tsp** salt
- **1 tsp** vanilla extract

Custard Filling (Krem Budyniowy)
- **500 ml (2 cups)** whole milk
- **150g (3/4 cup)** granulated sugar
- **2** egg yolks
- **50g (1/3 cup)** cornstarch
- **1 tsp** vanilla extract
- **200g (3/4 cup)** softened unsalted butter

Optional Topping
- Powdered sugar *(traditional)*

Instructions

Prepare the Choux Pastry
- Preheat the oven to **200°C (400°F)**. Line a 9x13 inch (23x33 cm) baking pan with parchment paper.
- In a saucepan, bring water, butter, and salt to a boil over medium heat.
- Remove from heat and quickly stir in the flour, mixing continuously until a smooth dough forms.
- Return to heat and cook for 1-2 minutes, stirring constantly, until the dough pulls away from the sides.
- Transfer to a mixing bowl and let cool for 5 minutes.
- Add eggs one at a time, beating well after each addition until the dough is smooth and glossy.
- Divide the dough into two equal portions. Spread one portion evenly into the baking pan.
- Bake for 25-30 minutes, until puffed and golden brown.
- Remove from the oven and let cool completely. Repeat with the second portion of dough.

Make the Custard Filling
- In a saucepan, heat 400ml (1¾ cups) of milk with sugar until warm (do not boil).
- In a separate bowl, whisk egg yolks, cornstarch, and the remaining 100ml (¼ cup) milk until smooth.
- Slowly pour the warm milk into the egg mixture while whisking constantly.
- Return to the saucepan and cook over low heat, stirring constantly, until thickened (about 5 minutes).
- Remove from heat, stir in vanilla extract, and let cool completely.
- Beat softened butter until fluffy, then gradually mix it into the cooled custard to create a smooth, creamy filling.

Assemble the Karpatka
- Place one layer of baked choux pastry on the bottom of a baking dish.
- Spread custard filling evenly over the pastry and cover with a second layer of choux pastry on top.
- Refrigerate for at least 2 hours or overnight.
- Dust with powdered sugar before serving.

Storage Tips
- Store in the refrigerator for up to 3 days.

Szarlotka
Polish Apple Pie

SERVES: 10 - 12   **PREP TIME:** 30 MINS   **COOKING TIME:** 45 MINS   **CHILLING TIME:** 30 MINS

Szarlotka was inspired by a French dessert called "Charlotte", which was popularized in Poland in the 19th century. Unlike American apple pie, Szarlotka is made with a buttery shortcrust or crumbly cake base and is served warm with whipped cream or vanilla ice cream.

Ingredients

For the Pastry (Ciastro Kruche)
- 300g (2½ cups) all-purpose flour
- 200g (7 oz) unsalted butter, cold and cubed
- 100g (½ cup) granulated sugar
- 1 large egg
- 1 tsp vanilla extract
- 1 tsp baking powder
- ¼ tsp salt

Apple Filling
- 1 kg (2.2 lbs) tart apples (e.g., Granny Smith, Antonówka, or Boskoop)
- 100g (½ cup) granulated sugar (adjust based on apple sweetness)
- 1 tsp ground cinnamon
- 1 tbsp lemon juice
- 1 tbsp potato starch or cornstarch

For the Topping
- Powdered sugar for dusting
- Streusel (crumb topping):
- 50g (¼ cup) unsalted butter
- 50g (⅓ cup) flour
- 50g (¼ cup) sugar

Instructions

Prepare the Shortcrust Pastry
- In a large bowl, mix flour, baking powder, sugar, and salt.
- Add cold butter cubes and rub them into the flour using your fingers or a pastry cutter until the mixture resembles coarse crumbs.
- Add the egg and vanilla extract, then knead the dough until it comes together (do not overwork it).
- Divide the dough into two portions (one slightly larger for the base).
- Wrap both in plastic wrap and chill for 30 minutes in the refrigerator.

Prepare the Apple Filling
- Peel, core, and slice the apples into thin slices or small chunks.
- Toss them with sugar, cinnamon, lemon juice, and starch.
- Cook over medium heat for about 5 minutes until slightly softened. Let cool.

Assemble the Szarlotka
- Preheat the oven to 180°C (350°F). Grease and line a 9-inch (23 cm) round or square baking pan with parchment paper.
- Roll out the larger portion of dough and press it into the bottom of the baking pan. Prick with a fork.
- Spread the apple filling evenly over the crust.
- Roll out the second portion of dough and place it over the apples (or crumble it over for a rustic look).
- Optional: If using streusel, mix the butter, flour, and sugar until crumbly and sprinkle on top.

Bake and Serve
- Bake for 40-45 minutes, until golden brown.
- Let cool before slicing.
- Dust with powdered sugar and serve warm or at room temperature.

Storage Tips
- Store at room temperature for 1 day, or in the fridge for up to 5 days.
- Can be frozen for up to 3 months. Wrap well in plastic wrap.

Metrowiec
Polish Layered "Meter Cake"

SERVES: 12 - 16   **PREP TIME:** 10 MINS   **BAKING TIME:** 40 MINS   **CHILLING TIME:** 2+ HOURS

The name "Metrowiec" comes from the fact that when the two long sponge cakes (one vanilla, one chocolate) are assembled in alternating slices, the finished cake can reach up to 1 meter in length!

Ingredients

For the Vanilla and Choc Sponge
- **6 large** eggs
- **50g (1¼ cups)** granulated sugar
- **250ml (1 cup)** vegetable oil
- **250ml (1 cup)** milk
- **400g (3¼ cups)** all-purpose flour
- **2 tsp** baking powder
- **2 tsp** vanilla extract
- **2 tbsp** cocoa powder

Cream Filling
- **500ml (2 cups)** whole milk
- **150g (¾ cup)** granulated sugar
- **50g (⅓ cup)** cornstarch
- **2** egg yolks
- **200g (¾ cup)** unsalted butter, softened
- **1 tsp** vanilla extract

For the Chocolate Glaze
- **100g (3.5 oz)** dark chocolate
- **50g (3 tbsp)** unsalted butter
- **2 tbsp** milk

Instructions

Prepare the Sponge Cakes
- Preheat oven to 180°C (350°F). Grease and line two loaf pans (25 cm / 10 inches each) with parchment paper.
- In a large bowl, beat eggs and sugar until pale and fluffy (about 5 minutes).
- Slowly add oil, milk, and vanilla extract, mixing continuously.
- Sift in flour and baking powder, mixing until smooth.
- Divide the batter into two equal portions:
  - One remains plain (vanilla layer).
  - To the other, mix in cocoa powder (chocolate layer).
- Pour each batter into a separate loaf pan and bake for 35-40 minutes, or until a toothpick inserted comes out clean.
- Let cool completely, then slice each cake into equal-sized strips (about 1-inch thick).

Prepare the Cream Filling
- In a saucepan, heat 400ml (1¾ cups) of milk with sugar until warm (do not boil).
- In a separate bowl, whisk cornstarch, egg yolks, and remaining 100ml (¼ cup) of milk until smooth.
- Slowly pour the warm milk into the egg mixture while whisking constantly.
- Return to the saucepan and cook over low heat, stirring until thickened (about 5 minutes).
- Remove from heat, stir in vanilla extract, and let cool.
- Beat softened butter until fluffy, then mix into the cooled custard to create a smooth, creamy filling.

Assemble the Metrowiec
- Lay a strip of vanilla sponge, spread a thin layer of cream, then place a chocolate sponge strip on top.
- Repeat the layers, alternating between vanilla and chocolate sponge strips, pressing gently so they stick together.
- Wrap in plastic wrap and refrigerate for at least 2 hours.

Prepare the Chocolate Glaze
- Melt chocolate, butter and milk over low heat until smooth.
- Pour over chilled cake and serve.
- Cut diagonally to reveal alternating layers.

Storage Tips
- Store in the fridge for up to 4 days.
- Can be frozen for up to 3 months (without glaze).

Ciasto Drozdzowe

Polish Yeast Cake

SERVES: 12 - 16   **PREP TIME:** 30 MINS   **RISING TIME:** 1.5 - 2 HRS   **BAKING TIME:** 35 - 40 MINS

Ciasto Drozdzowe is often called "the grandmother's cake" because it has been a traditional homemade treat for generations. It was usually baked for Sundays and holidays, filling homes with the aroma of warm vanilla, butter, and yeast.

Ingredients

For the Dough
- **500g (4 cups)** all-purpose flour
- **7g (2¼ tsp)** dry yeast (or 25g fresh)
- **200ml (¾ cup)** warm milk
- **100g (½ cup)** granulated sugar
- **100g (7 tbsp)** unsalted butter, melt
- **2 large** eggs
- **1 tsp** vanilla extract
- **½ tsp** salt

For the Crumb Topping (Kruszonka)
- **50g (⅓ cup)** all-purpose flour
- **50g (¼ cup)** granulated sugar
- **50g (3 tbsp)** unsalted butter, softened

Optional Add-Ins
- **Fruits:** Blueberries, plums, apples, raisins
- **Nuts:** Chopped almonds or walnuts
- **Powdered sugar** (for dusting)

Instructions

Prepare the Yeast Mixture
- **For dry yeast:** In a small bowl, mix warm milk (not hot!), 1 tbsp sugar, and yeast. Let sit for 10 minutes until foamy.
- **For fresh yeast:** Crumble the yeast into warm milk, add sugar, and let sit for 15 minutes.

Make the Dough
- In a large bowl, mix flour, sugar, and salt.
- Add yeast mixture, eggs, vanilla extract, and melted butter.
- Knead the dough for 10-15 minutes (by hand or with a mixer) until smooth and elastic.
- Cover with a clean towel and let rise in a warm place for 1-1.5 hours, or until doubled in size.

Prepare the Crumb Topping (Kruszonka)
- In a large bowl, mix flour, sugar, and salt.
- Add yeast mixture, eggs, vanilla extract, and melted butter.
- Knead the dough for 10-15 minutes (by hand or with a mixer) until smooth and elastic.
- Cover with a clean towel and let rise in a warm place for 1-1.5 hours, or until doubled in size.

Assemble the Cake
- Preheat oven to 180°C (350°F). Grease a 9x13 inch (23x33 cm) baking pan or a round springform pan.
- Punch down the risen dough and transfer it to the baking pan. Spread evenly.
- (Optional) Add fruits like plums, apples, or blueberries on top.
- Sprinkle with the crumb topping (kruszonka).

Bake the Cake
- Bake for 35-40 minutes, or until golden brown and a toothpick comes out clean.
- Let cool before slicing.

Serve
- Dust with powdered sugar.
- Serve warm or at room temperature with butter, jam, or honey.

Storage Tips
- Store covered at room temperature for 2 - 3 days, or in the fridge for 5 days.
- Can be frozen for up to 3 months.

Pischinger

Polish Wafer Cake with Chocolate Filling

SERVES: 12 - 16 **PREP TIME: 20 MINS** **CHILLING TIME: 2 HOURS** **BAKING TIME: 0 MIN**

Pischinger, the famous Polish wafer cake, was actually invented in Vienna in the 19th century by Oscar Pischinger, an Austrian confectioner. Families began making homemade versions using wafers layered with chocolate, caramel, or nut fillings. Today, Pischinger is a no-bake favorite, especially for holidays and special occasions!

Ingredients

For the Wafer Layers
- 5 large round or rectangular wafer sheets

For the Chocolate Filling
- **200g (7 oz)** dark chocolate, chopped
- **150g (⅔ cup)** unsalted butter
- **150g (¾ cup)** granulated sugar
- **2 tbsp** unsweetened cocoa powder
- **100ml (⅓ cup)** milk
- **100g (¾ cup)** ground nuts (hazelnuts, walnuts, or almonds) optional
- **1 tsp** vanilla extract

For the Chocolate Glaze
- **100g (3.5 oz)** dark chocolate, melted
- **2 tbsp** milk or cream
- **1 tbsp** butter

Instructions

Prepare the Chocolate Filling
- In a small saucepan over low heat, melt butter and sugar. Stir until dissolved.
- Add chopped chocolate, cocoa powder, and milk, stirring constantly until smooth.
- Remove from heat and mix in vanilla extract and ground nuts (if using).
- Let the mixture cool slightly until it thickens to a spreadable consistency.

Assemble the Wafer Cake
- Place one wafer sheet on a large flat surface or cutting board.
- Spread a thin, even layer of the warm chocolate filling over the wafer.
- Place the second wafer on top, pressing gently. Repeat the process with all wafers, leaving the top layer uncoated.
- Cover with parchment paper, place a lightweight object (like a cutting board) on top, and let it set in the fridge for at least 2 hours.

Add the Chocolate Glaze
- Melt chocolate, butter, and milk (or cream) over low heat, stirring until smooth.
- Let it cool slightly, then pour over the top wafer layer.
- Allow the glaze to set before slicing.

Serve
- Cut into triangles, squares, or rectangles.

Storage Tips
- Store in an airtight container at room temperature for up to 5 days.
- Refrigerate for a firmer texture or leave at room temperature for a softer bite.
- Customize by adding a rum or almond extract to the chocolate filling.

Plesniak

Polish Crumbly Cake with Jam and Meringue

| SERVES: 12 - 16 | PREP TIME: 30 MINS | CHILLING TIME: 20 MIN | BAKING TIME: 35 - 40 MINS |

The name "Plesniak" comes from the Polish word "pleśń," which means "mold"—but don't worry, there's no mold in this cake! The name refers to the cake's crumbly meringue topping, which resembles a textured, slightly "mottled" surface. This layered Polish dessert combines sweet, tart jam, a buttery shortcrust, and a crunchy meringue top, making it a delicious mix of textures and flavors!

Ingredients

For the Dough
- **400g (3⅓ cups)** all-purpose flour
- **200g (¾ cup)** unsalted butter, cold and cubed
- **100g (½ cup)** granulated sugar
- **5** egg yolks (save the whites)
- **1½ tsp** baking powder
- **1 tbsp** cocoa powder
- **1 tbsp** cold water (if needed)

For the Filling
- **300g (1¼ cups)** tart jam (blackcurrant, plum, or raspberry)

For the Meringue
- **5** egg whites
- **150g (¾ cup)** granulated sugar
- **1 tsp** vanilla extract

Instructions

Make the Shortcrust Dough
- In a large bowl, mix flour, sugar, and baking powder.
- Add cold butter and rub it into the flour with your fingers until it forms coarse crumbs.
- Add egg yolks and knead quickly into a dough. If too dry, add 1 tbsp cold water.
- Divide the dough into three equal parts:
  - Leave one plain.
  - Mix cocoa powder into the second portion for a chocolate layer.
  - Wrap both in plastic wrap and chill in the fridge for 30 minutes.
  - Freeze the third portion (it will be grated for the topping).

Assemble the Cake
- Preheat oven to 180°C (350°F). Grease a 9x13-inch (23x33 cm) baking pan.
- Roll out the plain dough and press it into the pan.
- Spread the tart jam evenly over the dough.
- Roll out the chocolate dough and carefully lay it over the jam.

Make the Meringue
- In a clean, dry bowl, beat egg whites with a mixer until soft peaks form.
- Gradually add sugar, beating until stiff and glossy.
- Stir in vanilla extract.

Bake the Cake
- Spread the meringue over the chocolate dough layer.
- Grate the frozen dough on top to create a crumbly texture.
- Bake for 40-45 minutes, until golden brown and crispy.
- Let cool.
- Dust with powdered sugar and serve.

Storage Tips
- Store at room temperature for 2 days or in the fridge for up to a week.
- Use a tart jam to balance the sweetness.
- Add chopped nuts for extra crunch.

Ciasto Stefanka
Polish Layered Honey Cake

SERVES: 12 - 16   PREP TIME: 40 MINS   BAKING TIME: 12 - 15 MINS PER LAYER   CHILLING TIME: 6 HOURS

Ciasto Stefanka, also known as "Miodownik" or honey cake, is sometimes called the "lazy cake" in Poland because it tastes even better the next day! The layers of honey cake soften as they absorb the cream filling, making the cake more moist and flavorful over time. Many families prepare it a day or two in advance for holidays and special occasions!

Ingredients

For the Honey Cake Layer
- 450g (3⅔ cups) all-purpose flour
- 150g (⅔ cup) granulated sugar
- 100g (7 tbsp) unsalted butter
- 3 tbsp honey
- 1 tsp baking soda
- 2 tbsp milk
- 2 eggs

For the Semolina Cream Filling
- 750ml (3 cups) milk
- 100g (½ cup) granulated sugar
- 100g (7 tbsp) unsalted butter
- 5 tbsp semolina (cream of wheat)
- 1 tsp vanilla extract

For the Chocolate Glaze (Optional)
- 100g (3.5 oz) dark chocolate
- 2 tbsp butter
- 2 tbsp milk or heavy cream

Instructions

Prepare the Honey Cake Dough
- In a small saucepan, melt butter, honey, and sugar over low heat. Stir until combined.
- Add baking soda mixed with milk, stir, and remove from heat.
- Let cool slightly, then mix in eggs.
- Gradually add flour, kneading until a smooth dough forms. It should be soft but not sticky.
- Divide into 3 equal portions, wrap in plastic, and let rest for 15 minutes.

Bake the Cake Layers
- Preheat oven to 180°C (350°F).
- Roll out each dough portion into a thin rectangle (about 9x13 inches / 23x33 cm).
- Place on a parchment-lined baking sheet and bake for 12-15 minutes, until golden brown.
- Let the layers cool completely. They will be hard but will soften after absorbing the filling.

Make the Semolina Cream
- In a saucepan, bring milk and sugar to a gentle boil.
- Gradually add semolina, whisking continuously to avoid lumps. Cook for 5-7 minutes, until thick.
- Remove from heat and let cool slightly.
- Beat in butter and vanilla extract, stirring until smooth.

Assemble the Cake
- Place one honey layer on a serving tray.
- Spread half of the semolina cream evenly over it.
- Place the second honey layer on top and spread the remaining cream.
- Cover with the third honey layer and gently press down.

Prepare the Glaze
- Melt chocolate, butter, and milk (or cream) over low heat, stirring until smooth.
- Pour over the top layer and spread evenly.

Chill and Serve
- Refrigerate overnight.

Storage Tips
- The cake gets better with time as the layers soften.
- Store in the fridge for up to 5 days.
- You can replace the semolina filling with pastry cream, dulce de leche, or buttercream.

Ciasto Izaura

Polish Chocolate Cheesecake Cake

SERVES: 12 - 16 **PREP TIME: 30 MINS** **BAKING TIME: 45 - 50 MINS** **COOLING TIME: 2+ HOURS**

Ciasto Izaura is sometimes called "Polish Brownie Cheesecake" because it combines a rich, fudgy chocolate cake base with a creamy cheesecake layer on top. The cake became popular in Poland during the 1980s, and its name was inspired by the Brazilian telenovela "Escrava Isaura", which was a huge hit in Poland at the time!

Ingredients

Chocolate Cake Layer
- 250g (2 cups) all-purpose flour
- 200g (1 cup) granulated sugar
- 200g (¾ cup) unsalted butter, soft
- 3 large eggs
- 3 tbsp unsweetened cocoa powder
- 100ml (⅓ cup) milk
- 2 tsp baking powder
- 1 tsp vanilla extract

Cheesecake Layer
- 500g (about 2¼ cups) Polish twaróg (or cream cheese, drained cottage cheese, or ricotta blended smooth)
- 100g (½ cup) granulated sugar
- 2 large eggs
- 1 tsp vanilla extract
- 1 tbsp cornstarch or potato starch
- 100g (7 tbsp) unsalted butter, softened

For the Chocolate Glaze (Optional)
- 100g (3.5 oz) dark chocolate
- 2 tbsp butter
- 2 tbsp milk or heavy cream

Instructions

Prepare the Chocolate Cake Batter
- Preheat oven to 180°C (350°F). Grease and line a 9x13-inch (23x33 cm) baking pan with parchment paper.
- In a large bowl, cream butter and sugar until fluffy.
- Add eggs, mixing well after each addition. Stir in vanilla extract.
- Sift in flour and stir to combine, then add cocoa powder and mix well.
- Add vanilla, mix until the batter is smooth and creamy.
- Spread batter evenly into the prepared pan.

Prepare the Cheesecake Layer
- In a separate bowl, beat the twaróg (or cream cheese) with sugar, eggs, and vanilla extract until smooth and creamy.
- Gently spoon this cheesecake mixture evenly over the chocolate cake batter.

Bake the Ciasto Lzaura
- Bake in the preheated oven (180°C/350°F) for 45-50 minutes, until a toothpick inserted into the chocolate part comes out clean and the cheesecake is set (it may jiggle slightly in the center).
- Remove from oven and let cool completely in the pan.

Prepare the Chocolate Glaze
- In a saucepan, gently heat chocolate, butter, and milk over low heat, stirring continuously until smooth.
- Allow to cool slightly, then spread evenly over the cooled cake.

Chill and Serve
- Chill the cake in the refrigerator for at least 2 hours (preferably overnight) to allow flavors to meld and texture to firm.
- 2. Cut into squares and serve chilled or at room temperature.

Storage Tips
- Store in an airtight container in the fridge for up to 4 days.
- To enhance flavor, add a teaspoon of lemon zest or a splash of rum to the cheesecake mixture.
- Can be made a day ahead—flavors intensify when rested overnight.

Ciasto Jogurtowe
Polish Yogurt Cake

SERVES: 10 - 12   **PREP TIME: 15 MINS**   **BAKING TIME: 40 - 45 MINS**   **COOLING TIME: 2+ HOURS**

Ciasto Jogurtowe "Yogurt cake" is often considered one of the easiest cakes to make in Poland because many traditional recipes use a yogurt cup as a measuring tool—no need for scales or measuring cups! This fluffy and moist cake is a popular everyday dessert, often served with powdered sugar, fruit, or a light glaze.

Ingredients

For the Yogurt Cake Batter
- **250g (2 cups)** all-purpose flour
- **200g (1 cup)** granulated sugar
- **3 large** eggs
- **250ml (1 cup)** plain yogurt
- **120ml (½ cup)** vegetable oil
- **2 tsp** baking powder
- **1 tsp** vanilla extract
- **½ tsp** salt
- **Zest** of 1 lemon (optional)

Optional Add-Ins
- **200g (1½ cups)** fresh or frozen berries (blueberries, raspberries, cherries)
- **Powdered sugar** (for dusting)
- **Lemon glaze** (powdered sugar + lemon juice)

Instructions

Prepare the Cake Batter
- Preheat oven to 180°C (350°F). Grease and line a 9-inch (23cm) round cake pan with parchment paper.
- In a large bowl, whisk together eggs and sugar until light and fluffy.
- Add yogurt, oil, vanilla extract, and lemon zest (if using). Whisk gently until smooth.
- In another bowl, sift together flour, baking powder, and salt.
- Gradually add the dry ingredients into the wet ingredients, mixing just until combined. Avoid overmixing.
- If using berries, gently fold them into the batter.

Bake the Cake
- Pour the batter into the prepared cake pan and smooth the top.
- Bake at 180°C (350°F) for 40-45 minutes, or until golden brown and a toothpick inserted into the center comes out clean.
- Allow the cake to cool in the pan for 10 minutes, then transfer it to a cooling rack to cool completely.

Serve
- Dust with powdered sugar before serving, or top with fresh berries.
- Serve warm or at room temperature with whipped cream.

Storage Tips
- Store at room temperature in an airtight container for up to 3 days.
- For longer freshness, store in the fridge (up to 5 days).
- Can be frozen for up to 3 months (wrap well before freezing).

Ciasto Zebra
Polish Zebra-Striped Cake

SERVES: 12 - 14 SLICES **PREP TIME:** 25 MINS **BAKING TIME:** 45 - 50 MINS **COOLING TIME:** 20 MIN

Ciasto Zebra gets its name from its striped black-and-white pattern, which resembles a zebra's coat! The cake is made by alternating layers of vanilla and chocolate batter, creating a beautiful marbled effect when sliced. It became a Polish household favorite in the 1980s and 1990s, especially because it looks impressive but is surprisingly easy to make!

Ingredients

For the Zebra Cake Batter
- **5 large** eggs, room temperature
- **250g (1¼ cups)** granulated sugar
- **250ml (1 cup)** vegetable oil
- **250ml (1 cup)** sparkling water or milk
- **375g (3 cups)** all-purpose flour
- **2½ tsp** baking powder
- **2 tbsp** unsweetened cocoa powder
- **1 tsp** vanilla extract
- **¼ tsp** salt

Optional Decoration
- **Powdered sugar** (for dusting)
- **Chocolate glaze** (optional)

Instructions

Prepare the Batter
- Preheat oven to 180°C (350°F). Grease and line a 9-inch (23 cm) round baking pan or springform pan.
- In a large bowl, whisk eggs and sugar together until pale and fluffy.
- Gradually add vegetable oil and sparkling water (or milk), whisking gently until well combined.
- Sift in flour and baking powder, gently folding until smooth and lump-free.

Divide Batter and Create Cocoa Mixture
- Divide batter evenly into two separate bowls.
- To one half, add vanilla extract and mix.
- To the other half, add cocoa powder and stir until completely incorporated.

Create the Zebra Stripes
- Using separate ladles or large spoons, pour 3 tablespoons of vanilla batter into the center of the prepared pan.
- Then pour 3 tablespoons of chocolate batter directly into the center of the vanilla batter.
- Alternate pouring batters this way (vanilla, then cocoa) repeatedly until both batters are used up.

Bake the Cake
- Bake in the preheated oven at 180°C (350°F) for 45-50 minutes, or until a toothpick inserted into the center comes out clean.
- Allow the cake to cool completely in the pan before removing and slicing.

Serve
- Dust the cake lightly with powdered sugar
- Slice the cake into wedges.
- Serve plain, or pair with whipped cream, chocolate sauce, or fresh berries for extra indulgence.

Storage Tips
- Store wrapped or in an airtight container at room temperature for up to 3 days or in the refrigerator for up to 5 days.

Ciasto Kokosowe

Polish Coconut Cake

| SERVES: 12 - 14 SLICES | PREP TIME: 30 MINS | BAKING TIME: 40 - 45 MINS | CHILL TIME: 2 HOURS |

Ciasto Kokosowe (Coconut Cake) became popular in Poland as coconut products became more available in the late 20th century. Since coconut wasn't traditionally grown in Poland, it was considered an exotic and luxurious ingredient. Today, this cake is a beloved treat, often topped with chocolate glaze or whipped cream, making it a delicious combination of tropical flavors and classic Polish baking!

Ingredients

Coconut Cake Layer
- **250g (2 cups)** all-purpose flour
- **200g (1 cup)** granulated sugar
- **200g (14 tbsp)** unsalted butter, soft
- **4 large** eggs
- **100ml (½ cup)** milk or coconut milk
- **2 tsp** baking powder
- **1 tsp** vanilla extract
- **½ tsp** salt
- **100g (1 cup)** shredded coconut

Coconut Cream Filling
- **400ml (1⅔ cups)** coconut milk or whole milk
- **100g (½ cup)** granulated sugar
- **2 tbsp** cornstarch
- **1 tsp** vanilla extract
- **150g (10 tbsp)** unsalted butter, softened
- **100g (1 cup)** shredded coconut

Topping - Optional
- **50g (½ cup)** shredded coconut (toasted lightly)

Instructions

Prepare the Coconut Cake
- Preheat oven to 180°C (350°F). Grease and line a 9x13-inch (23x33cm) baking pan with parchment paper.
- In a large bowl, cream butter and sugar until fluffy and pale.
- Add eggs, one at a time, mixing well.
- Stir in vanilla extract.
- In a separate bowl, combine flour, baking powder, salt, and shredded coconut.
- Gradually mix the dry ingredients into the butter mixture, alternating with milk (or coconut milk), stirring until the batter is smooth.
- Pour the batter evenly into the prepared baking pan.

Bake the Cake
- Bake at 180°C (350°F) for 40-45 minutes until golden brown, or a toothpick inserted in the center comes out clean.
- Allow to cool completely in the pan.

Prepare the Coconut Cream Filling
- In a saucepan, gently heat milk or coconut milk and sugar until hot but not boiling. Add coconut.
- In a separate bowl, mix cornstarch with 2 tbsp milk or water until smooth, then pour it into the coconut milk mixture.
- Cook on low heat, stirring continuously until thickened (about 3-5 minutes). Remove from heat and cool completely.
- Once cooled, beat softened butter with the coconut mixture until fluffy and creamy.

Assemble the Ciasto Kokosowe
- Simple: Spread the cream evenly over the top of the cooled cake.
- Layered: Carefully cut the cake horizontally into two layers, fill with half of the coconut cream, and then spread the rest on top.
- Sprinkle with lightly toasted shredded coconut to decorate.

Chill and Serve

Storage Tips
- Store the cake covered in the fridge for up to 5 days.
- For a richer coconut flavor, use coconut milk instead of regular milk in both the cake and cream.
- Toast shredded coconut lightly for the topping to enhance the flavor and texture.

Tort Makowy
Polish Poppy Seed Torte

SERVES: 12 SLICES **PREP TIME: 40 MINS** **BAKING TIME: 40 - 45 MINS** **CHILL TIME: 2 HOURS**

Tort Makowy (Poppy Seed Torte) is a symbol of good luck and prosperity in Poland! Poppy seeds have long been associated with wealth and fertility, which is why this cake is often served during Christmas (Wigilia) and special celebrations. Some Polish traditions even say that eating poppy seeds on New Year's Eve will bring good fortune in the coming year!

Ingredients

Poppy Seed Cake Layers
- **200g (1½ cups)** poppy seeds (ground)
- **150g (¾ cup)** granulated sugar
- **5 large** eggs, separated
- **100g (¾ cup)** ground almonds or walnuts
- **3 tbsp** all-purpose flour
- **50g (3½ tbsp)** unsalted butter, melted
- **1 tsp** baking powder
- **1 tsp** vanilla extract
- **½ tsp** almond extract (optional)
- **pinch** of salt

Custard Cream Filling
- **500ml (2 cups)** milk
- **150g (¾ cup)** granulated sugar
- **2 large** egg yolks
- **3 tbsp** cornstarch (or potato starch)
- **200g (¾ cup)** unsalted butter, softened
- **1 tsp** vanilla extract

Chocolate Glaze
- **100g (3.5 oz)** dark chocolate, chopped
- **2 tbsp** butter
- **3 tbsp** milk or heavy cream

Decoration (Optional)
- Sliced almonds or walnuts
- Fresh fruit or berries

Instructions

Prepare the Poppy Seed Cake Layers
- Preheat oven to 180°C (350°F). Grease and line two 9-inch (23 cm) round cake pans.
- In a large bowl, beat the egg yolks with half the sugar (75g) until pale and creamy.
- Mix in the finely ground poppy seeds gently until well combined.
- In a separate clean bowl, whisk egg whites with a pinch of salt until soft peaks form. Gradually add the remaining sugar (about half), whisking until stiff peaks form.
- Carefully fold the egg whites into the poppy seed mixture until combined (avoid deflating).
- Gently fold in the ground almonds (or walnuts) if using, ensuring a smooth batter.
- Divide batter evenly between the pans, smoothing the surface.
- Bake for 25-30 minutes or until firm and golden brown. Let cool completely.

Prepare the Custard Cream Filling
- Heat milk and sugar in a saucepan until steaming (do not boil).
- In a separate bowl, whisk egg yolks and cornstarch with 2 tablespoons milk until smooth.
- Gradually add hot milk to the yolk mixture, whisking continuously to prevent curdling.
- Return mixture to saucepan, cook over low heat, stirring constantly until thickened (5-7 minutes).
- Remove from heat, stir in vanilla extract, and let cool completely.
- Beat softened butter until fluffy, then gradually add cooled custard cream, beating until smooth.

Assemble the Cake
- Place one cooled cake layer onto a serving platter.
- Spread generously with custard cream filling.
- Place the second cake layer on top and gently press down.

Decorate, Chill and Serve

Storage Tips
- Store cake covered in the refrigerator for up to 4 days.
- Cake flavors intensify after refrigeration, making it perfect to bake a day ahead.
- For extra flavor, soak poppy seeds briefly in hot milk before grinding.

Miodownik
Traditional Polish Honey Cake

SERVES: 12 - 16 SLICES   PREP TIME: 40 MINS   BAKING TIME: 10 - 12 PER LAYER   CHILL TIME: 6 HOURS +

Miodowy, also known as Miodownik, is a traditional Polish honey cake that tastes better over time! The honey-infused layers absorb moisture from the cream filling, making the cake softer and more flavorful after a day or two. That's why many Polish families prepare it in advance for Christmas and special occasions, allowing it to develop its signature rich and tender texture!

Ingredients

Honey Cake Layers
- 500g (4 cups) all-purpose flour
- •150g (¾ cup) granulated sugar
- •150g (10½ tbsp) unsalted butter
- •3 tbsp honey
- •2 large eggs
- •1½ tsp baking soda
- •½ tsp salt

Custard Cream Filling
- 750ml (3 cups) whole milk
- 150g (¾ cup) granulated sugar
- 4 tbsp cornstarch (or potato starch)
- 2 large egg yolks
- 200g (14 tbsp) unsalted butter, softened
- 1 tsp vanilla extract

Chocolate Glaze
- 150g (5 oz) dark chocolate
- 3 tbsp butter
- 3 tbsp milk (or heavy cream)

Decoration (Optional)
- Chopped Walnuts or almonds

Instructions

Prepare Honey Cake Dough
- In a saucepan over low heat, gently melt butter, sugar, and honey, stirring continuously until smooth. Remove from heat and cool slightly.
- Add eggs and whisk vigorously until fully incorporated.
- Mix in baking soda (the mixture may foam slightly—this is normal).
- In a large bowl, sift flour and salt. Gradually pour the honey mixture into flour, mixing until a soft dough forms. Knead lightly until smooth (do not overwork).
- Divide dough into 3 equal portions, wrap in plastic, and refrigerate for 15-20 minutes.

Bake Honey Cake Layers
- Preheat oven to 180°C (350°F).
- Roll out each dough portion into thin rectangles (approximately 23x33 cm / 9x13 inch).
- Place each rolled dough on parchment-lined baking sheets and bake for 10 to 12 mins.

Prepare the Custard Cream Filling
- Heat milk and sugar in a saucepan until hot (do not boil).
- In a separate bowl, whisk egg yolks and cornstarch together with a small amount of cold milk until smooth.
- Gradually whisk the hot milk into the egg yolk mixture to temper, then return the mixture to the saucepan.
- Cook on low heat, stirring continuously until thickened (about 5 minutes). Remove from heat and let cool completely.
- Beat softened butter until fluffy, then gradually mix in cooled custard, adding vanilla extract. Beat until smooth.

Assemble the Miodownik
- Place one honey cake layer on a serving platter.
- Spread half of the custard filling evenly on top.
- Place second layer on top, spread remaining filling evenly.
- Place third layer on top and press gently.

Glaze, Decorate, and Chill Overnight Before Serving.

Storage Tips
- Store cake refrigerated, covered, for up to 5 days.
- This cake is best after resting overnight, as flavors deepen and layers soften.

Torcik Wedlowski
Polish Wedel Chocolate Wafer Cake

SERVES: 10 - 12   **PREP TIME: 25 MINS**   **CHILL TIME: 3 HOURS+ (BEST OVERNIGHT)**

Torcik Wedlowski is one of Poland's most iconic chocolate treats, first created by the famous Wedel chocolate company in the early 20th century. Each wafer cake is hand-decorated with chocolate swirls, making every piece unique! It's also a popular gift in Poland, often personalized with special messages written in chocolate

Ingredients

For the Wafer Layers
- 5-6 round wafer sheets (Polish wafle tortowe, available at Polish stores or online)

For the Chocolate-Hazelnut Cream
- 200g (7 oz) dark chocolate chopped
- 200g (1 cup) Nutella or similar chocolate-hazelnut spread
- 150g (⅔ cup) unsalted butter, soft
- 50g (¼ cup) powdered sugar
- 1 tsp vanilla extract
- 100g (¾ cup) finely chopped roasted hazelnuts

Chocolate Glaze
- 150g (5 oz) dark chocolate, chopped
- 3 tbsp heavy cream or milk
- 2 tbsp unsalted butter

Decoration (Optional)
- Chopped hazelnuts or almonds
- Chocolate shavings

Instructions

Prepare the Chocolate-Hazelnut Cream
- Melt the dark chocolate gently in a double boiler or microwave until smooth. Set aside to cool slightly.
- In a bowl, beat softened butter, powdered sugar, and vanilla extract until fluffy.
- Add Nutella and cooled melted chocolate, and beat until smooth and creamy.
- Fold in the finely chopped roasted hazelnuts (optional).

Assemble the Wafer Cake
- Place one wafer sheet onto a serving tray.
- Spread an even, thin layer of chocolate cream onto the wafer.
- Add another wafer sheet and repeat, layering cream and wafers until all wafers are used.
- (Note: Keep the top layer of wafer uncovered.)
- Press gently to seal layers firmly together

Prepare the Chocolate Glaze
- Melt dark chocolate, heavy cream, and butter gently over low heat until smooth.
- Let the glaze cool slightly until thick but still spreadable

Coat the Cake
- Spread the chocolate glaze evenly over the top and sides of the assembled wafer cake.
- Decorate immediately with hazelnuts, almonds, or chocolate shavings (optional).

Chill and Serve
- Refrigerate for at least 3 hours (best overnight) to allow layers to soften slightly and flavors to blend.
- Cut into small wedges or squares, and serve chilled or at room temperature.

Storage Tips
- Store covered in the refrigerator for up to 7 days.
- For an authentic Polish flavor, use high-quality dark chocolate (Wedel chocolate if available). Min 50% cocoa.
- Best prepared a day ahead for maximum flavor and ideal texture.

Ciasto z Rabarbarem
Polish Rhubarb Cake

SERVES: 12 - 14 **PREP TIME: 25 MINS** **BAKING TIME: 45 - 50 MINS** **CHILL TIME: 1 HOUR**

Ciasto z Rabarbarem (Rhubarb Cake) is a spring and summer favorite in Poland, as rhubarb is one of the first garden crops to ripen after winter! Traditionally, Polish grandmothers (babcie) would pick fresh rhubarb from their gardens and bake it into a sweet yet slightly tart cake, often topped with crumbly streusel (kruszonka) for extra texture.

Ingredients

For the Rhubarb Cake
- 300g (2½ cups) all-purpose flour
- 200g (1 cup) granulated sugar
- 200g (14 tbsp) unsalted butter, soft
- 4 large eggs
- 150ml (⅔ cup) milk
- 2 tsp baking powder
- 1 tsp vanilla extract
- pinch of salt

Rhubarb Layer
- 400g (3 cups) fresh rhubarb stalks, cleaned and sliced
- 2 tbsp sugar (for tossing with rhubarb)

Crumbly Topping (Kruszonka)
- 100g (¾ cup) all-purpose flour
- 60g (4 tbsp) unsalted butter, cold
- 50g (¼ cup) granulated sugar

Instructions

Prepare Rhubarb
- Wash and trim rhubarb stalks, removing leaves and tough ends.
- Slice rhubarb into small pieces (about 1-2 cm thick).
- Toss rhubarb slices with 2 tablespoons of sugar and set aside.

Prepare the Cake Batter
- **Preheat oven** to 180°C (350°F). Grease and line a **9x13-inch (23x33 cm)** baking pan with parchment paper.
- In a large bowl, cream **butter and sugar** until light and fluffy.
- Beat in **eggs**, one at a time, until thoroughly combined. Stir in **vanilla extract**.
- In a separate bowl, sift together **flour, baking powder, and salt**.
- Gently mix the dry ingredients into the butter mixture, alternating with the **milk**, until the batter is smooth and creamy.

Assemble the Cake
- Spread batter evenly into the prepared baking pan.
- Sprinkle the prepared rhubarb evenly over the cake batter, lightly pressing it in.

Prepare the Crumbly Topping
- In a bowl, combine **flour, sugar, and cold butter**.
- Rub together with your fingers until the mixture resembles coarse crumbs.
- Sprinkle evenly over the rhubarb layer.

Bake the Cake
- Bake in the preheated oven at **180°C (350°F)** for **45-50 minutes**, or until golden brown and a toothpick inserted into the center comes out clean.
- Remove from oven and let cool completely before slicing.

Serve
- Cut into squares and serve dusted lightly with powdered sugar (optional).
- Delicious served warm or at room temperature.

Storage Tips
- Store covered at room temperature for up to 2 days or refrigerated for up to 5 days.
- Add strawberries or apples for additional flavor variations.
- Serve with whipped cream or vanilla ice cream for a special touch.

Ciasto Krówkowe
Polish Caramel Cake

SERVES: 12 - 14 **PREP TIME:** 40 MINS **BAKING TIME:** 45 - 50 MINS **CHILLING TIME:** 3+ HOURS

Ciasto Krówkowe (Caramel Cake) is inspired by Krówki, Poland's famous soft caramel fudge! The word "krówka" means "little cow" in Polish, referencing the cow-themed wrappers of these beloved sweets.

Ingredients

For the Sponge Cake Layers
- 5 large eggs, separated
- 150g (¾ cup) granulated sugar
- 150g (1¼ cups) all-purpose flour
- 50g (3½ tbsp) unsalted butter, melted and cooled
- 1 tsp vanilla extract
- pinch of salt

For the Caramel Cream
- 1 can (400g/14 oz) sweetened condensed milk (or ready-made Polish caramel spread)
- 250g (1 cup + 2 tbsp) unsalted butter, softened
- 1 tsp vanilla extract
- pinch of salt

For the Caramel Glaze
- 100g (½ cup) sugar
- 50g (3½ tbsp) butter
- 100ml (⅓ cup + 1 tbsp) heavy cream
- pinch of salt

Decoration
- Chopped walnuts or almonds
- Polish caramel candies (krówki), chopped

Instructions

Bake the Sponge Cake
- Preheat oven to 180°C (350°F). Grease and line a 9-inch (23cm) round cake pan.
- Beat egg whites with salt until stiff peaks form. Set aside.
- In a separate bowl, whisk egg yolks with sugar until thick and pale.
- Gently fold egg whites into yolks mixture, alternating with sifted flour, until smooth.
- Carefully fold in cooled melted butter and vanilla extract.
- Pour batter into prepared pan, bake for 25-30 minutes, or until golden and a toothpick comes out clean and cool completely before slicing.

Prepare the Caramel Cream
- Beat **softened butter** until fluffy.
- Add the ready-made **caramel spread (masa krówkowa)** or homemade boiled caramel (cooled completely), vanilla extract, and pinch of salt. Beat until creamy and smooth.

Assemble the Cake
- Place the first cake layer on a serving plate.
- Spread generously with caramel cream.
- Repeat with remaining layers, finishing with cream on the top layer and sides, smoothing neatly.

Prepare the Caramel Glaze
- In a saucepan, gently melt **sugar** over medium heat until caramelized (golden brown).
- Carefully add **butter and cream**, stirring continuously until smooth (be careful; mixture may bubble vigorously).
- Remove from heat, add a pinch of salt, and let cool slightly before use.

Decorate the Cake
- Drizzle caramel glaze over the assembled cake, allowing it to drip down the sides attractively.
- Decorate with **chopped walnuts, almonds, or caramel candies (krówki)**.

Chill for 3 hours or overnight and serve.

Storage Tips
- Store cake refrigerated for up to 5 days.
- Cake tastes best after chilling overnight, allowing caramel flavors to blend thoroughly.
- For easier preparation, purchase ready-made Polish caramel cream (masa krówkowa).

Piernik
Traditional Polish Gingerbread Cake

SERVES: 12 - 16 SLICES **PREP TIME:** 30 MINS **BAKING TIME:** 50 - 60 MINS **RESTING TIME:** 24 HOURS

Piernik (Polish gingerbread) has been a staple in Poland for over 700 years! The city of Toruń became famous for its pierniki in the Middle Ages, and these spiced honey cakes were so prized that they were even used as diplomatic gifts for kings and nobles. Some traditional Toruń gingerbread molds date back to the 16th century, featuring intricate carvings of knights, royalty, and mythical creatures!

Ingredients

For the Gingerbread Cake
- **500g (4 cups)** all-purpose flour
- **250g (1¼ cups)** honey
- **200g (1 cup)** granulated sugar
- **200g (14 tbsp)** unsalted butter
- **4 large** eggs
- **100ml (⅓ cup + 1 tbsp)** milk
- **2 tsp** baking soda
- **1 tsp** baking powder
- **1 tsp** cinnamon
- **1 tsp** ground ginger
- **½ tsp** ground cloves
- **½ tsp** ground nutmeg
- **¼ tsp** salt
- **1 tbsp** cocoa powder *(optional, deepens color & flavor)*

For the Filling
- **300g (1¼ cups)** Polish plum butter *(powidła śliwkowe)* or apricot jam

For the Chocolate Glaze
- **100g (3½ oz)** dark chocolate, chopped
- **3 tbsp** heavy cream
- **1 tbsp** unsalted butter

Decoration
- Chopped walnuts or almonds
- Candied orange peel

Instructions

Prepare the Honey Mixture
- In a saucepan, melt together butter, honey, and sugar over medium-low heat, stirring continuously until sugar dissolves. Remove from heat and cool to room temperature.

Prepare the Cake Batter
- Preheat oven to 170°C (340°F). Grease and line a 9x13-inch (23x33 cm) baking pan or two loaf pans.
- Transfer cooled honey mixture to a mixing bowl. Add eggs one at a time, whisking thoroughly after each.
- Mix in milk until smooth.
- In a separate bowl, combine flour, baking soda, baking powder, cocoa powder (if using), spices, and salt.
- Gradually add dry ingredients into the honey mixture, stirring gently until fully combined (batter will be thick).

Bake the Cake
- Pour batter evenly into the prepared pan(s), smoothing the top.
- Bake for 50-60 minutes until a toothpick comes out clean from the center.
- Allow cake(s) to cool completely before removing from the pan.
- (Traditional Tip: Allow cake to rest covered overnight to intensify flavors.)

Assemble the Piernik
- Carefully slice the cooled gingerbread horizontally into two even layers.
- Spread an even layer of plum butter or jam between the cake layers.
- Gently press layers together.

Prepare the Glaze
- In a small saucepan, gently melt **chocolate, cream, and butter** over low heat, stirring until glossy and smooth.
- Allow to cool slightly before glazing.

Decorate and Serve

Storage Tips
- Store wrapped at room temperature or in the refrigerator for up to 7 days.
- Piernik improves in flavor and texture after resting; it's ideal to make a day or two in advance.

Keks
Traditional Polish Fruitcake

SERVES: 12 - 14   **PREP TIME:** 20 MINS   **BAKING TIME:** 50 - 60MINS   **RESTING TIME:** 1 HOUR

Keks, the Polish version of fruitcake, was once considered a luxury dessert because dried fruits and nuts were expensive and hard to find in Poland. Traditionally, it was baked only for special occasions like Christmas and Easter, making it a festive treat! Today, it remains a popular holiday dessert, often soaked in rum or brandy for extra flavor.

Ingredients

Cake Batter
- 250g (2 cups) all-purpose flour
- 200g (1 cup) granulated sugar
- 200g (14 tbsp) unsalted butter, soft
- 4 large eggs
- 2 tsp baking powder
- 1 tsp vanilla extract
- ½ tsp almond extract (optional)
- Pinch of salt

Fruit and Nut Mix
- 150g (1 cup) mixed candied fruit peel (orange, lemon, citron)
- 100g (¾ cup) dried fruits (raisins, cranberries, cherries, apricots, chopped dates)
- 50g (⅓ cup) chopped walnuts or almonds
- 2 tbsp all-purpose flour (to coat fruit and nuts)

Optional Decoration
- Powdered sugar for dusting

Instructions

Prepare the Fruit and Nuts
- Combine candied fruits, dried fruits, and chopped nuts in a bowl.
- Sprinkle 2 tablespoons of flour over the fruit and nut mixture and stir well to coat evenly. (This prevents them from sinking in the batter.)

Make the Cake Batter
- Preheat oven to 170°C (340°F). Grease and line a loaf pan (23x13 cm / 9x5 inches) or round cake pan with parchment paper.
- In a large mixing bowl, cream softened butter and sugar until fluffy and pale.
- Beat in eggs, one at a time, mixing thoroughly after each addition.
- Stir in vanilla and almond extracts.
- In a separate bowl, sift together flour, baking powder, and salt.
- Gently fold dry ingredients into the butter-egg mixture until combined, creating a smooth batter.

Combine Batter with Fruits
- Fold the flour-coated fruit and nut mixture into the batter, mixing gently until evenly distributed.

Bake the Keks
- Pour batter evenly into prepared baking pan and smooth the top.
- Bake in the preheated oven for 50-60 minutes, or until golden brown and a toothpick inserted into the center comes out clean.
- Allow cake to cool in the pan for 15 minutes before transferring to a wire rack to cool completely.

Decorate and Serve
- Dust generously with powdered sugar before serving.

Storage Tips
- Keks improves in flavor and moisture when stored for a day or two wrapped in parchment and foil.
- Store at room temperature for up to 5 days or refrigerate for longer shelf life (up to 2 weeks).
- You can soak dried fruit in a bit of brandy or rum overnight for extra flavor.

Ciasto Budyniowe
Polish Pudding Cake

SERVES: 12 - 14 **PREP TIME: 25 MINS** **BAKING TIME: 40 - 45 MINS** **CHILLING TIME: 2+ HOURS**

Ciasto Budyniowe (Pudding Cake) is loved for its silky-smooth custard filling, which is made using budyń—Poland's favorite vanilla or chocolate pudding mix! Budyń has been a childhood staple for generations, often served warm as a simple dessert. Incorporating it into cake recipes became a popular way to add a creamy, rich texture to traditional Polish bakes!

Ingredients

Cake Batter
- **250g (2 cups)** all-purpose flour
- **150g (¾ cup)** granulated sugar
- **150g (10½ tbsp)** unsalted butter, soft
- **3 large** eggs
- **2 tsp** baking powder
- **1 tsp** vanilla extract
- **100ml (⅓ cup + 2 tbsp)** milk
- **Pinch** of salt

Vanilla Pudding (Budyn) Filling
- **500ml (2 cups)** milk
- **50g (¼ cup)** granulated sugar
- **1 packet (40g / about 4 tbsp)** vanilla pudding powder (budyń) or substitute with cornstarch
- **1 tsp** vanilla extract

Streusel (Kruszonka) Topping
- **100g (¾ cup)** all-purpose flour
- **60g (4 tbsp)** unsalted butter, cold
- **50g (¼ cup)** granulated sugar

Instructions

Prepare the Vanilla Pudding Filling
- Mix vanilla pudding powder (or cornstarch) with ½ cup cold milk until smooth.
- In a saucepan, heat the remaining milk with sugar and vanilla extract until steaming (not boiling).
- Gradually whisk pudding mixture into the hot milk. Cook on low heat, stirring continuously, until thickened (3-4 minutes).
- Remove from heat and set aside to cool slightly.

Prepare the Cake Batter
- Preheat oven to 180°C (350°F). Grease and line a 9x13-inch (23x33 cm) baking pan.
- In a bowl, cream butter and sugar.
- Beat in eggs, one at a time, then mix in vanilla extract.
- In a separate bowl, sift together flour, baking powder, and salt.
- Alternately fold flour mixture and milk into the butter mixture until combined into a smooth batter.

Assemble the Cake
- Spread the batter evenly into the prepared pan.
- Gently spoon the prepared vanilla pudding evenly on top of the cake batter, creating a smooth, even layer.

Prepare Streusel
- Mix flour, sugar, and cold butter using fingertips or a pastry cutter until it resembles coarse crumbs.
- Sprinkle the kruszonka evenly over the pudding layer.

Bake the Cake
- Bake in the preheated oven (180°C/350°F) for 45-50 minutes, or until golden brown and set.
- Allow cake to cool completely in the pan.

Serve
- Slice the cake into squares.
- Serve chilled or at room temperature, dusted with powdered sugar (optional).

Storage Tips
- Store the cake refrigerated in an airtight container for up to 4 days.
- For authentic taste, use Polish vanilla pudding mix (budyń).
- Add seasonal fruits (cherries, strawberries, raspberries, blueberries) under the pudding layer for extra flavor.

Fale Dunaju
Polish "Danube Waves" Layered Cake

SERVES: 12 - 16 **PREP TIME:** 40 MINS **BAKING TIME:** 45 MINS **CHILLING TIME:** 3 - 4 HOURS

Fale Dunaju (Danube Waves Cake) gets its name from the wavy pattern created by the sinking fruit and the marbled layers of vanilla and chocolate cake. The design is meant to resemble the gentle waves of the Danube River, which flows through Central and Eastern Europe.

Ingredients

For the Cake Layers
- **250g (2 cups)** all-purpose flour
- **200g (1 cup)** granulated sugar
- **200g (14 tbsp)** unsalted butter, soft
- **4 large** eggs
- **2 tsp** baking powder
- **2 tbsp** unsweetened cocoa powder
- **1 tsp** vanilla extract
- **½ tsp** salt
- **4 tbsp** milk

Fruit Layer
- **400g (14oz)** canned or fresh cherries, pitted and drained

Buttercream Custard Filling
- **500ml (2 cups)** whole milk
- **100g (½ cup)** granulated sugar
- **1 packet (40g)** vanilla pudding powder *(or substitute with 4 tbsp cornstarch and extra vanilla)*
- **200g (14 tbsp)** unsalted butter, soft
- **1 tsp** vanilla extract

Chocolate Glaze
- **150g (5 oz)** dark chocolate
- **2 tbsp** butter
- **3 tbsp** heavy cream

Instructions

Prepare the Cake Batter
- Preheat oven to 180°C (350°F). Grease and line a 9x13-inch (23x33 cm) baking pan.
- Cream butter and sugar until fluffy. Beat in eggs one at a time, then stir in vanilla extract.
- In a separate bowl, sift flour, baking powder, and salt.
- Gradually mix dry ingredients into the butter mixture, alternating with milk, until batter is smooth.

Create the Layers
- Divide batter into **two equal portions**.
- Mix **cocoa powder** thoroughly into one half of the batter, leaving the other half vanilla.
- Spread the **vanilla batter** evenly into the prepared pan first.
- Carefully spread the **chocolate batter** evenly over the vanilla batter.

Add Cherries
- Scatter drained cherries evenly across the chocolate batter layer.

Bake the Cake
- Bake at 180°C (350°F) for 30-35 minutes, until cake is set and a toothpick inserted in the center comes out clean.
- Cool completely in the pan.

Prepare Buttercream Custard Filling
- In a saucepan, whisk together milk, sugar, vanilla, and cornstarch. Cook over low heat, stirring constantly, until thickened (about 5 minutes). Cool completely.
- Beat softened butter until fluffy, gradually adding the cooled custard cream. Beat until smooth and creamy.

Assemble Cake
- Spread buttercream evenly over the cooled cake. Smooth out the surface and refrigerate for 1 hour.

Prepare Chocolate Glaze, Decorate and Chill
- Melt chocolate, butter, and cream gently in a saucepan, stirring continuously until smooth.
- Cool slightly before using.

Cut and Serve
- Cut into squares or rectangles to reveal the characteristic "Danube waves."

Storage Tips
- Store covered in the refrigerator for up to 5 days.
- Make the cake a day ahead; flavors improve overnight.

Ciasto Cytrynowe
Polish Lemon Cake

SERVES: 10 - 12 SLICES   PREP TIME: 20 MINS   BAKING TIME: 45 - 50 MINS   CHILLING TIME: 3 - 4 HOURS

Ciasto Cytrynowe (Lemon Cake) became especially popular in Poland as a refreshing alternative to heavier, cream-filled cakes, making it a favorite for spring and summer gatherings. In traditional Polish baking, lemon zest and juice are often used to enhance flavors, as fresh lemons were once considered a luxury ingredient and were highly valued in Polish kitchens!

Ingredients

For the Lemon Cake
- **250g (2 cups)** all-purpose flour
- **200g (1 cup)** granulated sugar
- **200g (14 tbsp)** unsalted butter, soft
- **4 large** eggs
- **2 tsp** baking powder
- Zest of **2 lemons**
- Juice of **1 lemon (about 3 tbsp)**
- **100ml (⅓ cup + 2 tbsp)** milk
- **½ tsp** salt
- **1 tsp** vanilla extract

For the Lemon Glaze
- **150g (1 cup)** powdered sugar
- Juice of **1** lemon **(about 2-3 tbsp)**

Decoration (Optional)
- **Extra lemon zest**
- **Fresh berries** (blueberries, raspberries)

Instructions

Prepare the Lemon Cake Batter
- Preheat oven to 180°C (350°F). Grease and line a 9x5-inch (23x13 cm) loaf pan or round cake pan.
- Cream butter and sugar until pale and fluffy.
- Add eggs one at a time, beating thoroughly.
- Mix in lemon zest, lemon juice, and vanilla extract.
- In a separate bowl, sift together flour, baking powder, and salt.
- Gradually fold dry ingredients into butter-egg mixture, alternating with the milk, until batter is smooth and well-combined.

Bake the Cake
- Pour batter evenly into the prepared pan and smooth the surface.
- Bake at 180°C (350°F) for 45-50 minutes, or until golden brown and a toothpick inserted in the center comes out clean.
- Allow cake to cool in the pan for 10 minutes, then transfer to a wire rack to cool completely.

Prepare the Lemon Glaze
- In a small bowl, whisk together powdered sugar and lemon juice until smooth.
- (Adjust consistency by adding more sugar or lemon juice as needed.)

Glaze and Decorate
- Once the cake is cooled, drizzle evenly with lemon glaze, allowing it to drip down the sides.
- Decorate with extra lemon zest or fresh berries, if desired.

Serve

Storage Tips
- Store the cake covered at room temperature for up to 3 days, or refrigerated for up to 5 days.

Tort Orzechowy
Polish Walnut Torte

SERVES: 12 SLICES **PREP TIME: 40 MINS** **BAKING TIME: 35 - 40 MINS** **CHILLING TIME: 3+ HOURS**

In Polish tradition, walnuts are believed to symbolize wisdom and abundance, making Tort Orzechowy a cake often served at weddings, birthdays, and anniversaries to bring good luck and prosperity to guests!

Ingredients

Walnut Sponge Layers
- **200g (1½ cups)** ground walnuts
- **100g (¾ cup)** all-purpose flour
- **200g (1 cup)** granulated sugar
- **6 large** eggs, separated (egg whites and yolks divided)
- **1 tsp** baking powder
- **1 tsp** vanilla extract
- **Pinch** of salt

Cream Filling
- **250g (1 cup + 2 tbsp)** unsalted butter, soft
- **150g (¾ cup)** powdered sugar
- **1 tsp** vanilla extract
- **3 tbsp** milk (optional, for creaminess)
- **100g (¾ cup)** finely chopped walnuts (optional)

Chocolate Glaze (Optional)
- **150g (5 oz)** dark chocolate, chopped
- **3 tbsp** heavy cream
- **2 tbsp** unsalted butter

Decoration (Optional)
- Walnuts (whole or chopped)
- Chocolate shavings

Instructions

Prepare the Walnut Sponge Cake
- Preheat oven to 180°C (350°F). Grease and line two 9-inch (23 cm) round cake pans.
- In a bowl, beat egg yolks with half the sugar until pale and fluffy. Stir in vanilla extract.
- Combine ground walnuts and flour in another bowl and gently fold into yolk mixture.
- In a separate bowl, beat egg whites with remaining sugar until stiff peaks form.
- Gently fold egg whites into walnut mixture, maintaining airiness.
- Divide batter between the prepared pans evenly and smooth the tops.

Bake the Sponge Cake
- Bake for 25–30 minutes until golden and firm, and a toothpick inserted into the center comes out clean.
- Cool completely on a wire rack before assembling.

Prepare the Walnut Buttercream Filling
- Beat softened butter until creamy and fluffy.
- Gradually add powdered sugar, vanilla extract, and milk (optional). Beat until smooth and creamy.
- Stir in finely chopped walnuts (optional, for extra nutty flavor).

Assemble the Tort Orzechowy
- Place the first sponge layer on a serving plate.
- Spread generously with walnut buttercream filling.
- Place the second layer on top and press gently.

Prepare Chocolate Glaze
- Melt chocolate, butter, and cream or milk gently over low heat, stirring until glossy.
- Let cool slightly before pouring evenly over the top of the cake, letting it drip down the sides attractively.

Decorate and Serve
- Decorate with extra walnuts or chocolate shavings, as desired.
- Chill the cake in the refrigerator for at least 2 hours (preferably overnight) to develop flavors.

Storage Tips
- Store covered in the refrigerator for up to 4 days.
- The cake tastes best when allowed to sit overnight to absorb the cream fully.
- Add a splash of brandy or rum to the buttercream for extra depth of flavor.

Wuzetka
Polish Chocolate Layer Cake

| SERVES: 12 SLICES | PREP TIME: 40 MINS | BAKING TIME: 30 MINS | CHILLING TIME: 1 HOUR |

Wuzetka is one of Poland's most famous cakes, often referred to as Warsaw's signature dessert. Some believe the "W-Z" in the name comes from the Warsaw East-West Route (Trasa W-Z) built after WWII, making it a piece of Polish history in cake form!

Ingredients

Chocolate Sponge Cake
- **6 large** eggs
- **150g (¾ cup)** granulated sugar
- **120g (1 cup)** all-purpose flour
- **30g (¼ cup)** unsweetened cocoa powder
- **1 tsp** baking powder
- **1 tsp** vanilla extract
- **Pinch** of salt

Whipped Cream Filling
- **500ml (2 cups)** heavy whipping cream (cold)
- **50g (¼ cup)** powdered sugar
- **1 tsp** vanilla extract
- **2 tsp gelatin + 2 tbsp** warm water (optional, for stability)

Chocolate Glaze
- **100g (3.5 oz)** dark chocolate
- **50g (3 tbsp)** unsalted butter
- **2 tbsp** milk

Syrup (for soaking)
- **100ml (½ cup)** strong brewed coffee or black tea
- **1 tbsp** sugar

Instructions

Prepare the Chocolate Sponge Cake
- Preheat oven to 180°C (350°F). Grease and line a 9x13 inch (23x33 cm) baking pan with parchment paper.
- In a bowl, beat eggs, sugar, and vanilla extract until pale and fluffy (about 5 minutes).
- Sift together flour, cocoa powder, baking powder, and salt. Gradually fold into the egg mixture using a spatula.
- Pour batter into the pan, smooth the top, and bake for 25–30 minutes until a toothpick inserted comes out clean.
- Let the cake cool completely, then cut it horizontally into two layers.

Prepare the Whipped Cream Filling
- In a small bowl, dissolve gelatin in warm water (if using) and let cool.
- Whip heavy cream, powdered sugar, and vanilla extract until soft peaks form.
- If using gelatin, slowly pour it in while mixing on low speed.

Assemble the Whipped Cream Filling
- In a small bowl, dissolve gelatin in warm water (if using) and let cool.
- Whip heavy cream, powdered sugar, and vanilla extract until soft peaks form.
- If using gelatin, slowly pour it in while mixing on low speed.

Assemble the Wuzetka Cake
- Place one cake layer on a serving tray. Brush with coffee syrup if using.
- Spread whipped cream evenly over the first layer.
- Place the second cake layer on top, pressing gently. Chill for 30 minutes.

Prepare Chocolate Glaze
- Melt chocolate, butter, and milk over low heat, stirring until smooth.
- Pour warm glaze over the cake, smoothing with a spatula.

Chill and Serve
- Refrigerate for at least 30 minutes before slicing.
- Cut into squares

Storage Tips
- Store in an airtight container in the refrigerator for up to 3 days.
- The cake tastes even better the next day as flavors develop.

Chapter Two

Cookies & Small Sweets (Ciastka i Słodycze)

Pączki
Traditional Polish Doughnuts

SERVES: 20 - 24   **PREP TIME:** 30 + 60 MINS   **COOKING TIME:** 20 MINS   **RESTING TIME:** 1.5 - 2 HOURS

In Poland, the Thursday before Lent is known as "Tłusty Czwartek" (Fat Thursday). On this day, Poles eat millions of pączki—often jokingly claiming it brings bad luck to not eat at least one!

Ingredients

For the Dough
- **500g (4 cups)** all-purpose flour, plus extra for dusting
- **250ml (1 cup)** warm milk
- **7g (2¼ tsp)** active dry yeast (or 25g fresh yeast)
- **70g (⅓ cup)** granulated sugar
- **4 large** egg yolks
- **60g (4 tbsp)** unsalted butter, melted
- **1 tsp** vanilla extract
- **½ tsp** salt
- **1 tbsp** vodka or rum (optional, helps reduce oil absorption)
- Vegetable oil for frying **(approx. 1 liter/4 cups)**

Fillings
- Fruit jam (raspberry, plum, rose hip)
- Custard/chocolate cream
- Sweetened cheese (twaróg)

Decoration
- Powdered sugar for dusting
- Granulated sugar
- Glaze (powdered sugar + milk)
- Candied fruits

Instructions

Prepare the Dough
- In a bowl, combine warm milk, yeast, and 1 tbsp sugar. Let sit for 10 minutes until frothy.
- In a large mixing bowl, combine flour, remaining sugar, and salt.
- Add egg yolks, yeast mixture, and optional rum or vanilla extract.
- Knead dough, gradually adding softened butter, until smooth and elastic (about 10 minutes). Dough should be soft, slightly sticky, but manageable.
- Cover dough with a cloth and let rise in a warm place until doubled in size (1–1½ hours).

Shape the Doughnuts
- On a floured surface, roll dough to 1-inch thickness.
- Using a round cutter or glass (about 3 inches/7 cm diameter), cut dough into circles.
- Place circles on parchment-lined trays, cover loosely, and let rise again for 30-45 minutes until puffed.

Fry the Pączki
- Heat oil to 175°C (350°F) in a large pot or deep fryer.
- Carefully place doughnuts in hot oil, frying 2–3 minutes per side, until puffed and golden.
- Drain fried doughnuts on paper towels.

Fill the Pączki
- Allow doughnuts to cool slightly.
- Using a piping bag or pastry syringe, inject filling into each doughnut (fruit jam, custard, chocolate cream, etc.).

Serve
- Dust with powdered sugar or drizzle with glaze.

Storage Tips
- Pączki taste best freshly made; consume within 1–2 days.
- Store leftovers in an airtight container at room temperature.
- Add vodka or rum to the dough to reduce oil absorption, creating lighter doughnuts.

Faworki (Chrusciki)
Polish Angel Wings

SERVES: 30 - 40 PIECES **PREP TIME: 30 MINS** **COOKING TIME: 20 MINS** **RESTING TIME: 30 MINS**

In Poland, there's a fun tradition of testing the crispiness of Faworki by listening for a distinct "crunch" sound when breaking them—the louder and lighter the crunch, the better they are considered to be!

Ingredients

For the Dough
- **250 g (2 cups)** all-purpose flour
- **5** egg yolks
- **3 tbsp** sour cream
- **1 tbsp** vodka or rum (optional, helps create a crispier texture)
- **1 tbsp** granulated sugar
- **Pinch** of salt
- Vegetable oil for frying **(about 1 liter/4 cups)**

For Decoration
- Powdered sugar *(for dusting generously)*

Instructions

Prepare the Dough
- In a large bowl, whisk together egg yolks, sugar, vanilla extract, and salt.
- Add sour cream, mixing thoroughly.
- Gradually add the flour, kneading until a smooth, elastic dough forms. If dough feels dry, add 1 tablespoon cold water.
- Knead for 8–10 minutes until dough is smooth and elastic. (Traditional tip: hit the dough firmly with a rolling pin to create an airy texture.)
- Wrap dough in plastic wrap and let rest at room temperature for 30 minutes.

Shape the Faworki
- Divide dough into two portions. Roll out each portion to 2 mm (very thin) thickness.
- Cut dough into rectangles (about 3x10 cm / 1x4 inches).
- Make a small slit lengthwise in the center of each rectangle.
- Pull one end of the rectangle through the slit to form the characteristic twisted shape.

Fry the Faworki
- In a deep pot or fryer, heat vegetable oil to 175°C (350°F).
- Fry Faworki in small batches for 30–60 seconds per side, turning once until lightly golden.
- Drain briefly on paper towels to remove excess oil.

Serve
- Allow Faworki to cool slightly, then dust liberally with powdered sugar.
- Serve immediately for maximum crispness.

Storage Tips
- Faworki taste best the day they're fried, but you can store leftovers in an airtight container at room temperature for up to 3 days.
- For extra crispiness, ensure dough is rolled very thinly (almost transparent).

Kruche Ciasteczka
Polish Butter Cookies

SERVES: 30 COOKIES **PREP TIME: 20 MINS** **COOKING TIME: 12 - 15 MINS** **RESTING TIME: 30 MINS**

In Poland, families traditionally bake these buttery cookies around holidays, especially Christmas and Easter, involving children in shaping and decorating them—a beloved family tradition passed down through generations.

Ingredients

For the Cookies
- **300 g (2½ cups)** all-purpose flour
- **200 g (14 tbsp)** unsalted butter, cold and cubed
- **100 g (½ cup)** granulated sugar
- **2** large egg yolks
- **1 tsp** vanilla extract
- Pinch of salt

Decoration (Optional)
- Powdered sugar (for dusting)
- Chocolate glaze (melted chocolate + butter)
- Jam (raspberry, apricot, strawberry) for filling or sandwiching

Instructions

Prepare the Dough
- In a large bowl, mix the flour, sugar, and salt.
- Add the cold butter (cut into small cubes) and rub it into the flour with your fingertips until the mixture resembles coarse breadcrumbs.
- Add the egg yolks and vanilla extract, and knead briefly to form a smooth dough. (Avoid overmixing.)
- Wrap dough in plastic wrap and refrigerate for at least 30 minutes.

Shape the Cookies
- Preheat oven to 180°C (350°F). Line baking trays with parchment paper.
- On a lightly floured surface, roll dough out to approximately ½ cm (¼-inch) thickness.
- Cut out cookies using cookie cutters of your choice.
- Transfer cookies to prepared baking sheets.

Bake the Cookies
- Bake at 180°C (350°F) for 12–15 minutes until lightly golden at the edges.
- Cool cookies on a wire rack completely before decorating.

Decorate & Serve
- Dust generously with powdered sugar or decorate with chocolate glaze or jam, if desired.
- Serve with tea, coffee, or milk.

Storage Tips
- Store cookies in an airtight container at room temperature for up to 1 week.
- The dough can be prepared in advance and refrigerated overnight.

Kokosanki
Polish Coconut Macaroons

SERVES: 20 - 24 COOKIES **PREP TIME: 15 MINS** **BAKING TIME: 15 - 20 MINS** **RESTING TIME: 20 MINS**

In Poland, Kokosanki are affectionately nicknamed "snowballs," especially during the holiday season, due to their white coconut appearance resembling snowy winter scenes.

Ingredients

For the Dough
- **200g (2½ cups)** unsweetened shredded coconut
- **3 large** egg whites
- **150g (¾ cup)** granulated sugar
- **1 tsp** vanilla extract
- **Pinch of salt**

For Decoration (Optional)
- Dark chocolate

Instructions

Prepare the Coconut Mixture
- Preheat oven to **170°C (340°F)**. Line a baking sheet with parchment paper.
- In a bowl, whisk egg whites with a pinch of salt until soft peaks form.
- Gradually add sugar, whisking continuously until glossy, stiff peaks form.
- Gently fold in shredded coconut and vanilla extract until fully combined.

Shape and Bake Kokosanki
- Using two spoons or a small scoop, form tablespoon-sized balls of mixture.
- Place them onto the prepared baking sheet, spaced about 2 cm apart.
- Bake at **170°C (340°F) for 15–20 minutes**, until golden brown and crispy on the outside.

Cool and Decorate
- Allow cookies to cool on the baking sheet for 5 minutes before transferring to a wire rack.
- Optionally, drizzle or dip the bottom of Kokosanki in melted dark chocolate for added flavor.

Storage Tips
- Store in an airtight container at room temperature for up to 1 week.
- For extra flavor, add lemon zest or almond extract to the coconut mixture.

Ciasteczka Serowe
Polish Cheese Cookies

SERVES: 30 COOKIES **PREP TIME: 20 MINS** **BAKING TIME: 15 - 20 MINS** **RESTING TIME: 20 MINS**

In Polish tradition, cheese-based cookies like Ciasteczka Serowe symbolize hospitality and warmth. Serving these treats to guests is a delightful way to show Polish hospitality and generosity!

Ingredients

For the Dough
- **250g (2 cups)** all-purpose flour
- **200g (7 oz)** Polish farmer's cheese (twaróg) or cream cheese, softened
- **200g (14 tbsp)** unsalted butter, cold and cubed
- **2 tbsp** powdered sugar
- **1 tsp** vanilla extract
- Pinch of salt

For Decoration
- Powdered sugar

Instructions

Prepare the Dough
- In a large bowl, combine flour, softened twaróg (or cream cheese), and softened butter.
- Knead gently until dough forms a soft, smooth ball. (Do not overwork.)
- Wrap dough in plastic wrap and refrigerate for 30 minutes to chill.

Shape the Cookies
- Preheat oven to **180°C (350°F)** and line a baking tray with parchment paper.
- On a lightly floured surface, roll out dough to approximately **5 mm (¼-inch)** thickness.
- Cut into circles (approx. 6–7 cm / 2½ inches diameter) using a round cutter or glass.
- Fold each circle into halves, then quarters, pressing gently to maintain shape *(traditional shaping style)*. Alternatively, you can bake them as simple rounds.

Bake the Cookies
- Place cookies on a baking tray lined with parchment paper, spaced about 2 cm apart.
- Bake in a preheated oven at 180°C (350°F) for 15–20 minutes, until lightly golden at the edges.
- Cool cookies completely on a wire rack.

Serve
- Generously dust with **powdered sugar** while cookies are still warm or cooled.

Storage Tips
- Store cookies in an airtight container at room temperature for up to 4–5 days.
- For added flavor, mix lemon zest or vanilla extract into the dough.
- You may also fill these cookies with jam for extra sweetness.

Ciasteczka Miodowe
Polish Honey Cookies

| SERVES: 30 COOKIES | PREP TIME: 20 MINS | BAKING TIME: 10 - 12 MINS | RESTING TIME: 30 MINS |

In Poland, Ciasteczka Miodowe symbolize sweetness and prosperity, and are traditionally baked during Christmas and gifted to friends and family as tokens of good wishes and happiness for the coming year!

Ingredients

For the Dough
- **300g (2½ cups)** all-purpose flour
- **150g (½ cup)** honey (preferably a mild-flavored honey)
- **100g (7 tbsp)** unsalted butter, softened
- **100g (½ cup)** granulated sugar
- **1 large** egg
- **1 tsp** baking soda
- **1 tsp** vanilla extract
- **1 tsp** cinnamon
- **½ tsp** ground ginger
- **Pinch** of ground cloves (optional)
- Pinch of salt

Decoration
- Powdered sugar (for dusting)
- Chocolate glaze or icing

Instructions

Prepare the Dough
- In a bowl, cream together softened butter and granulated sugar until pale and fluffy.
- Add the egg, honey, and vanilla extract, mixing thoroughly until combined.
- In a separate bowl, combine flour, baking soda, cinnamon, ginger, cloves (if using), and salt.
- Gradually mix the dry ingredients into the wet mixture until it forms a soft dough.
- Wrap the dough in plastic wrap and chill in the refrigerator for about 30 minutes (this helps the cookies hold shape and improves texture).

Shape the Cookies
- Preheat oven to 180°C (350°F). Line baking sheets with parchment paper.
- Roll out the chilled dough on a lightly floured surface to approximately 5 mm (¼ inch) thickness.
- Use cookie cutters to cut out shapes (hearts, stars, circles, or festive shapes).
- Transfer cookies to prepared baking sheets.

Bake the Cookies
- Bake cookies at 180°C (350°F) for 10–12 minutes, or until edges turn golden brown.
- Allow cookies to cool on the baking sheet briefly before transferring to a wire rack to cool completely.

Decorate and Serve
- Dust generously with powdered sugar or drizzle with chocolate glaze or icing.
- Serve alongside tea, coffee, or milk.

Storage Tips
- Store in an airtight container at room temperature for up to 1–2 weeks.
- Cookies soften and develop richer flavor when stored for a day or two before eating.

Ciasteczka Maślane
Polish Butter Cookies

SERVES: 30 COOKIES   **PREP TIME:** 20 MINS   **BAKING TIME:** 12 - 15 MINS   **RESTING TIME:** 30 MINS

In Poland, baking butter cookies (Ciasteczka Maślane) is often a family activity, especially around Christmas. Children traditionally join their parents or grandparents to decorate cookies, turning it into a beloved yearly family event filled with joyful memories.

Ingredients

For the Dough
- **250 g (2 cups)** all-purpose flour
- **200 g (14 tbsp)** unsalted butter, softened
- **100 g (½ cup)** granulated sugar
- **2** large egg yolks
- **1 tsp** vanilla extract
- **Pinch of salt**

Decoration
- Powdered sugar (for dusting)
- Jam, chocolate, or nuts

Instructions

Prepare the Dough
- In a large bowl, cream butter and sugar until pale and fluffy.
- Add the egg yolks and vanilla extract, mixing until smooth.
- Gradually add flour and mix gently until a soft dough forms.
- Wrap dough in plastic wrap and refrigerate for about 30 minutes (this makes shaping easier).

Shape the Cookies
- Preheat oven to 180°C (350°F). Line baking trays with parchment paper.
- Roll dough on a lightly floured surface to about ½ cm (¼ inch) thickness.
- Using cookie cutters, cut into desired shapes.
- Place cookies onto parchment-lined baking trays, leaving some space between each.

Bake the Cookies
- Bake at 180°C (350°F) for 12–15 minutes, until lightly golden around the edges.
- Cool cookies briefly on trays, then transfer to wire racks to cool completely.

Decorate and Serve
- Dust with powdered sugar, drizzle with chocolate glaze, or sandwich pairs with fruit jam, if desired.
- Serve alongside tea, coffee, or milk.

Storage Tips
- Store cookies in an airtight container at room temperature for up to 7 days.
- Add lemon zest or almond extract to the dough for extra flavor.

Ciasteczka Orzechowe
Polish Nut Cookies

SERVES: 30 COOKIES **PREP TIME: 20 MINS** **BAKING TIME: 12 - 15 MINS** **RESTING TIME: 30 MINS**

In Poland, it's common to bake Ciasteczka Orzechowe during family gatherings, with each household proudly using their own special blend of nuts—making each batch unique and often becoming a treasured family recipe passed through generations!

Ingredients

For the Dough
- **200 g (1½ cups)** all-purpose flour
- **150 g (10½ tbsp)** unsalted butter, softened
- **100 g (½ cup)** granulated sugar
- **100 g (¾ cup)** ground walnuts (or almonds, hazelnuts)
- **1 large** egg yolk
- **1 tsp** vanilla extract
- **Pinch** of salt

Decoration
- Powdered sugar (for dusting)
- Whole or chopped nuts for topping

Instructions

Prepare the Dough
- In a large bowl, cream butter and sugar until pale and fluffy.
- Add the egg yolk and vanilla extract, mixing well.
- Stir in flour and ground nuts, mixing gently until a soft dough forms.
- Wrap dough in plastic wrap and refrigerate for 30 minutes to firm up.

Shape the Cookies
- Preheat oven to 180°C (350°F). Line baking trays with parchment paper.
- Roll dough into small balls (walnut-sized) and place on baking trays, spacing them about 3 cm (1 inch) apart.
- Gently flatten each cookie slightly with your palm or a fork.
- Optional: Press a nut on top of each cookie for decoration.

Bake the Cookies
- Bake in preheated oven at 180°C (350°F) for 12–15 minutes or until lightly golden.
- Allow cookies to cool for 5 minutes on trays before transferring to a wire rack to cool completely.

Decorate and Serve
- Dust with powdered sugar or drizzle with melted chocolate if desired.
- Serve alongside coffee, tea, or milk.

Storage Tips
- Store in an airtight container at room temperature for up to 1 week.
- For variety, experiment with different nuts or a combination of walnuts, almonds, and hazelnuts.

Ciasteczka Amerykanki
Polish "American-Style" Cookies

SERVES: 16 - 20 COOKIES   **PREP TIME: 20 MINS**   **BAKING TIME: 15 - 18 MINS**   **RESTING TIME: 30 MINS**

In Poland, these cookies are affectionately known as "American Cookies," but ironically, most Americans have never tasted or even heard of this particular Polish treat! Their charming name reflects Poland's fascination with American culture during the mid-20th century.

Ingredients

For the Cookies
- **300 g (2½ cups)** all-purpose flour
- **100 g (½ cup)** granulated sugar
- **100 g (7 tbsp)** unsalted butter, softened
- **2 large** eggs
- **100 ml (⅓ cup + 2 tbsp)** milk
- **2 tsp** baking powder
- **1 tsp** vanilla extract
- **Pinch** of salt

Icing for Decoration
- **150g (1 cup)** powdered sugar
- **2–3 tbsp** warm water or lemon juice
- Chocolate glaze (optional alternative)

Instructions

Prepare the Batter
- Preheat oven to 180°C (350°F). Line baking trays with parchment paper.
- In a bowl, cream together softened butter and sugar until fluffy.
- Add eggs one at a time, mixing thoroughly. Stir in vanilla extract.
- In a separate bowl, mix flour, baking powder, and salt.
- Alternately add dry ingredients and milk to butter mixture, mixing gently to form a smooth, thick batter.

Bake the Cookies
- Using a tablespoon or ice cream scoop, place rounded portions of batter onto baking sheets lined with parchment paper, spacing cookies about 4 cm (1½ inches) apart.
- Bake at 180°C (350°F) for 15–18 minutes, until lightly golden around edges.
- Allow cookies to cool on a wire rack before icing.

Prepare and Add Icing
- Mix powdered sugar with warm water, stirring until smooth and creamy.
- Spread icing evenly over cooled cookies, allowing it to set completely before serving.

Storage Tips
- Store cookies in an airtight container at room temperature for up to 4–5 days.
- Add lemon zest or cocoa powder to the icing for extra flavor variations.

Ciasteczka Migdałowe
Polish Almond Cookies

SERVES: 25 COOKIES **PREP TIME: 20 MINS** **BAKING TIME: 12 - 15 MINS** **RESTING TIME: 30 MINS**

In Poland, almonds symbolize good luck, prosperity, and fertility, making Ciasteczka Migdałowe a traditional gift or treat served at weddings and family celebrations!

Ingredients

For the Cookies
- **200 g (1½ cups)** almond flour (ground almonds)
- **150 g (1¼ cups)** all-purpose flour
- **150 g (10½ tbsp)** unsalted butter, soft
- **120 g (⅔ cup)** granulated sugar
- **1 large** egg
- **1 tsp** almond extract
- **½ tsp** vanilla extract
- **Pinch** of salt

Decoration (Optional)
- Whole almonds (blanched or sliced)
- Powdered sugar (for dusting)

Instructions

Prepare the Dough
- In a large bowl, cream softened butter and sugar until pale and fluffy.
- Add egg, almond extract, and vanilla extract; mix thoroughly.
- Combine almond flour, all-purpose flour, and salt separately, then gradually fold into butter mixture until a soft dough forms.
- Wrap dough in plastic wrap and refrigerate for 30 minutes to firm slightly.

Shape the Cookies
- Preheat oven to 180°C (350°F). Line baking trays with parchment paper.
- Roll dough into small walnut-sized balls and place them on trays spaced 3 cm (1 inch) apart.
- Gently flatten each cookie slightly with your palm. Decorate with whole almonds pressed gently into the center (optional).

Serve and Decorate
- Dust cookies with powdered sugar before serving (optional).
- Enjoy with tea, coffee, or milk.

Storage Tips
- Store cookies in an airtight container at room temperature for up to 1 week.
- For extra almond flavor, toast almond flour lightly before mixing into the dough.

Ciasteczka z Dżemem
Polish Jam-Filled Cookies

SERVES: 25 - 30 COOKIES **PREP TIME: 20 MINS** **BAKING TIME: 15 - 20 MINS** **RESTING TIME: 30 MINS**

In Poland, these jam-filled cookies are affectionately called "oczka," meaning "little eyes," because the colorful jam peeking through resembles bright, cheerful eyes!

Ingredients

For the Cookie Dough
- **300g (2½ cups)** all-purpose flour
- **200g (14 tbsp)** unsalted butter, softened
- **100g (½ cup)** granulated sugar
- **2 large** egg yolks
- **1 tsp** vanilla extract
- **Pinch** of salt

Filling
- Fruit jam (raspberry, plum, apricot, strawberry) about 200g (¾ cup)

Decoration
- Powdered Sugar (for dusting)

Instructions

Prepare the Dough
- In a large bowl, cream butter and sugar until light and fluffy.
- Add egg yolks and vanilla extract, mixing thoroughly.
- Gradually add flour and salt, mixing until a soft dough forms.
- Wrap dough in plastic wrap and chill in the refrigerator for 30 minutes.

Shape the Cookies
- Preheat oven to 180°C (350°F). Line baking trays with parchment paper.
- Roll dough to about 5 mm (¼ inch) thickness on a lightly floured surface.
- Use cookie cutters to cut out circles (6-7cm)
- In half of the circles, cut out a smaller shape in the center (hearts, circles, stars, etc.).
- Place whole circles onto trays, add ½–1 teaspoon jam to the center, and top with the cut-out dough circles, pressing edges lightly to seal.

Bake the Cookies
- Bake cookies at 180°C (350°F) for 12–15 minutes until edges turn lightly golden.
- Cool on a wire rack.

Decorate and Serve
- Dust generously with **powdered sugar**.
- Allow to cool fully before serving.

Storage Tips
- Store cookies in an airtight container at room temperature for up to 1 week.
- Use thick, quality jams for best results (Polish plum jam—powidła śliwkowe—is particularly traditional).

Makówki
Traditional Polish Poppy Seed Dessert

SERVES: 8 - 10 **PREP TIME: 20 MINS** **COOKING TIME: 20 MINS** **CHILLING: 2+ HOURS**

In the region of Silesia, Poland, Makówki is traditionally served during Christmas Eve dinner (Wigilia). It's believed that eating poppy seed desserts brings prosperity, happiness, and good luck for the coming year!

Ingredients

For the Dessert
- **200 g (1½ cups)** poppy seeds (ground or finely milled)
- **500 ml (2 cups)** whole milk
- **150 ml (⅔ cup)** honey (or sugar)
- **100 g (¾ cup)** raisins or dried cranberries
- **100 g (¾ cup)** chopped walnuts or almonds
- **100 g (½ cup)** dried fruits (raisins, apricots, figs), chopped
- **1 tsp** vanilla extract
- **½ tsp** ground cinnamon (optional but recommended)
- **Pinch** of salt

Bread Layers
- **8–10 slices** of white bread, sweet bread rolls (chałka), or brioche, sliced thickly

Decoration (Optional)
- Slivered almonds
- Extra raisins or dried fruit

Instructions

Prepare the Poppy Seed Mixture
- Grind poppy seeds finely (best soaked overnight beforehand for tenderness).
- In a saucepan, combine milk, sugar, vanilla extract, and cinnamon; bring to a gentle simmer.
- Stir in ground poppy seeds, dried fruits, and nuts. Cook gently for 10–15 minutes, stirring frequently, until thick and creamy. Remove from heat and cool slightly.

Assemble the Makowki
- Slice bread or rolls into 1 cm (½-inch) thick slices.
- In a deep serving dish or bowl, layer slices of bread alternately with warm poppy seed mixture, beginning and ending with poppy seed mixture.
- Repeat layers until all ingredients are used.

Chill and Serve
- Allow Makówki to cool at room temperature, then refrigerate for at least 4 hours or overnight for flavors to develop fully.
- Serve chilled, garnished with almonds, walnuts, raisins, or dried fruits.

Storage Tips
- Store refrigerated, covered, up to 3 days.
- Use challah or brioche rolls for a sweeter, richer version.
- Adjust sweetness by adding more or less sugar according to preference.

Ciasteczka Marmurkowe
Polish Marble Cookies

SERVES: 25 - 30 COOKIES   **PREP TIME:** 20 MINS   **BAKING TIME:** 12 - 15 MINS   **RESTING TIME:** 30 MINS

The beautiful marble pattern of Ciasteczka Marmurkowe symbolizes unity and harmony, making them especially popular for family gatherings, celebrations, and weddings in Poland!

Ingredients

Vanilla Dough
- **200g (1½ cups)** all-purpose flour
- •**100g (7 tbsp)** unsalted butter, softened
- •**100g (½ cup)** granulated sugar
- •**1 large** egg
- •**1 tsp** vanilla extract
- •**Pinch of salt**

Chocolate Dough
- **200g (1½ cups)** all-purpose flour
- **100g (7 tbsp)** unsalted butter, softened
- **100g (½ cup)** granulated sugar
- **1 large** egg
- **2 tbsp** unsweetened cocoa powder
- **Pinch of salt**

Instructions

Prepare the Vanilla Dough
- 1. Cream butter and sugar until fluffy.
- 2. Add egg, vanilla extract, and salt. Mix well.
- 3. Fold in flour gradually, forming a soft dough. Set aside.

Prepare the Chocolate Dough
- 1. Cream butter and sugar until fluffy.
- 2. Add egg, salt, and mix.
- 3. Stir in flour and cocoa powder until combined into a smooth dough.

Shape and Bake the Cookies
- Roll each dough into a long cylinder shape of equal length.
- 2. Gently twist the two doughs together, folding lightly to create a marble effect.
- 3. Roll gently to form a combined cylinder, wrap in plastic wrap, and refrigerate for 30 minutes.

Shape and Bake Cookies
- Preheat oven to 180°C (350°F). Line baking sheets with parchment paper.
- Slice chilled dough into 1 cm (½ inch) thick slices.
- Place cookies on baking trays spaced about 2 cm apart.
- Bake at 180°C (350°F) for 12–15 minutes, until edges are lightly golden.
- Cool on wire racks.

Serve
- Enjoy cookies plain or dusted lightly with powdered sugar.

Storage Tips
- Store cookies in an airtight container at room temperature for up to 1 week.
- Dough can be prepared ahead and refrigerated or frozen.

Ciasteczka Cytrynowe
Polish Lemon Cookies

SERVES: 25 - 30 COOKIES　　**PREP TIME: 20 MINS**　　**BAKING TIME: 12 - 15 MINS**　　**RESTING TIME: 30 MINS**

In Poland, lemon cookies are often served during springtime celebrations, symbolizing freshness, renewal, and new beginnings, especially around Easter!

Ingredients

Cookie Dough
- **250g (2 cups)** all-purpose flour
- **150g (10½ tbsp)** unsalted butter, softened
- **100g (½ cup)** granulated sugar
- **1 large** egg
- **Zest of 1** large lemon
- **2 tbsp** fresh lemon juice
- **1 tsp** vanilla extract
- **Pinch** of salt

Lemon Glaze
- **120g (1 cup)** powdered sugar
- **2–3 tbsp** fresh lemon juice

Instructions

Prepare the Dough
- In a bowl, cream butter and sugar until fluffy.
- Add the egg, lemon zest, lemon juice, and vanilla extract, mixing well.
- Gradually mix in flour and salt until a soft dough forms.
- Chill dough for 30 minutes wrapped in plastic wrap.

Shape and Bake the Cookies
- Preheat oven to 180°C (350°F). Line baking sheets with parchment paper.
- Roll dough into small balls and place on trays, slightly flattening each.
- Bake for 12–15 minutes until lightly golden around edges.
- Allow to cool completely.

Decorate and Serve
- Combine powdered sugar and lemon juice to form glaze. Drizzle over cooled cookies and let set.
- Serve cookies with tea, coffee, or milk.
- Perfect as an afternoon treat or festive dessert.

Storage Tips
- Store cookies airtight at room temperature for up to 1 week.
- For more intense flavor, add extra lemon zest or lemon extract.

Ciasteczka Piernikowe
Polish Spiced Gingerbread Cookies

SERVES: 30 COOKIES   **PREP TIME: 25 MINS + 1 HOUR CHILLING**   **BAKING TIME: 10 - 12 MINS**

In Poland, traditionally, Piernikowe cookies were often hung on the Christmas tree as edible decorations. Children loved this tradition, eagerly awaiting permission to eat the beautifully decorated ornaments!

Ingredients

Cookie Dough
- **350g (2¾ cups)** all-purpose flour
- • **150g (½ cup)** honey
- • **100g (7 tbsp)** unsalted butter, softened
- • **100g (½ cup)** granulated sugar
- • **1 large egg**
- • **1 tsp** baking soda
- • **2 tsp** ground cinnamon
- • **1 tsp** ground ginger
- • **½ tsp** ground nutmeg
- • **½ tsp** ground cloves (optional)
- • **pinch of salt**

Icing (Optional)
- 150g (1 cup) powdered sugar
- 2 tbsp lemon juice (or water)

Instructions

Prepare the Dough
- In a bowl, cream together softened butter and sugar until fluffy.
- Add egg, honey, and mix thoroughly.
- Combine flour, baking soda, spices, and salt separately.
- Gradually mix dry ingredients into wet mixture until a smooth dough forms.
- Wrap dough in plastic wrap and chill for 30–60 minutes.

Shape and Bake the Cookies
- Preheat oven to 180°C (350°F). Line trays with parchment paper.
- Roll dough to approximately 5 mm (¼-inch) thickness on a floured surface.
- Cut cookies into desired shapes using festive cookie cutters.
- Bake cookies at 180°C (350°F) for 10–12 minutes, until lightly golden.
- Cool on wire racks completely.

Decorate and Serve
- Decorate cookies with icing made from powdered sugar mixed with lemon juice or water.
- Allow icing to dry completely before serving.

Storage Tips
- Store cookies airtight at room temperature up to 2 weeks.
- Cookies become softer and more flavorful after resting for a day or two.

Ciasteczka Kakaowe
Polish Cocoa Cookies

SERVES: 25 COOKIES   **PREP TIME: 20 MINS**   **BAKING TIME: 12 - 15 MINS**

In Poland, traditionally, Piernikowe cookies were often hung on the Christmas tree as edible decorations. Children loved this tradition, eagerly awaiting permission to eat the beautifully decorated ornaments!

Ingredients

Cookie Dough
- **250g (2 cups)** all-purpose flour
- **150g (10½ tbsp)** unsalted butter, softened
- **100g (½ cup)** granulated sugar
- **3 tbsp** unsweetened cocoa powder
- **1 large egg**
- **1 tsp** vanilla extract
- **Pinch of salt**

Decoration (Optional)
- Powdered sugar for dusting
- Melted chocolate for drizzling

Instructions

Prepare the Dough
- In a bowl, cream butter and sugar until fluffy.
- Add egg and vanilla extract, mixing thoroughly.
- Gradually blend in flour, cocoa powder, and salt until a soft dough forms.
- Chill dough in the refrigerator for 30 minutes.

Shape and Bake Cookies
- Preheat oven to 180°C (350°F). Line baking sheets with parchment paper.
- Roll dough into walnut-sized balls, place on trays, and slightly flatten each with a fork or palm.
- Bake for 12–15 minutes until edges firm up.
- Allow cookies to cool completely on a wire rack.

Decorate and Serve
- Dust generously with powdered sugar or drizzle with melted chocolate (optional).
- Enjoy with tea, coffee, or milk.

Storage Tips
- Store cookies in an airtight container at room temperature for up to 1 week.
- Add chocolate chips or chopped nuts for extra flavor.

Ciasteczka Cynamonowe
Polish Cinnamon Cookies

SERVES: 25 - 30 COOKIES **PREP TIME: 20 MINS** **BAKING TIME: 12 - 15 MINS**

In Polish folklore, cinnamon symbolizes warmth and prosperity. Polish families often bake Ciasteczka Cynamonowe during the holidays to fill their homes with the welcoming scent of cinnamon, believed to bring good luck and happiness!

Ingredients

Cookie Dough
- **250g (2 cups)** all-purpose flour
- **150g (10½ tbsp)** unsalted butter, softened
- **100g (½ cup)** granulated sugar
- **2 tsp** ground cinnamon
- **1 large** egg
- **1 tsp** vanilla extract
- **Pinch** of salt

Topping (Optional)
- Cinnamon sugar (2 tbsp sugar mixed with 1 tsp cinnamon)
- Powdered sugar for dusting

Instructions

Prepare the Dough
- Cream butter and sugar in a bowl until fluffy.
- Mix in egg and vanilla extract thoroughly.
- Gradually add flour, ground cinnamon, and a pinch of salt, mixing gently until a smooth dough forms.
- Wrap dough in plastic wrap and refrigerate for 30 minutes to firm.

Shape and Bake Cookies
- Preheat oven to 180°C (350°F). Line baking trays with parchment paper.
- Roll dough out on a lightly floured surface to approximately 5 mm (¼ inch) thickness.
- Cut cookies into desired shapes using cookie cutters.
- Sprinkle tops with cinnamon sugar (optional) before baking.
- Bake for 12–15 minutes until lightly golden at edges.

Decorate and Serve
- Cool cookies on wire racks, then dust with powdered sugar if desired.
- Enjoy warm or at room temperature with tea, coffee, or milk.

Storage Tips
- Store in an airtight container at room temperature for up to 1 week.
- Cookies become more flavorful and aromatic after resting a day or two.

Ciasteczka Waniliowe
Polish Vanilla Cookies

SERVES: 25 - 30 COOKIES   **PREP TIME: 20 MINS**   **BAKING TIME: 12 - 15 MINS**

In Poland, vanilla cookies (Ciasteczka Waniliowe) are often prepared as simple gifts or tokens of appreciation, especially during Christmas and Easter, symbolizing warmth, friendship, and family bonds!

Ingredients

Cookie Dough
- **250g (2 cups)** all-purpose flour
- **150g (10½ tbsp)** unsalted butter, softened
- **100g (½ cup)** granulated sugar
- **1 large** egg
- **2 tsp** vanilla extract (or seeds from 1 vanilla bean)
- **Pinch** of salt

Decoration (Optional)
- Powdered sugar for dusting

Instructions

Prepare the Dough
- Cream butter and sugar until pale and fluffy.
- Add the egg, vanilla extract, and a pinch of salt, mixing well.
- Gradually mix in flour until a soft dough forms.
- Wrap dough in plastic wrap and chill for about 30 minutes.

Shape and Bake Cookies
- Preheat oven to 180°C (350°F). Line baking trays with parchment paper.
- Roll dough on a lightly floured surface to 5 mm (¼-inch) thickness.
- Cut cookies into desired shapes using cookie cutters.
- Transfer cookies onto prepared baking trays.
- Bake at 180°C (350°F) for 12–15 minutes, until lightly golden.

Decorate and Serve
- Cool cookies completely on a wire rack.
- Dust generously with powdered sugar if desired.
- Enjoy with tea, coffee, or milk.

Storage Tips
- Store cookies airtight at room temperature for up to 1 week.
- For a richer vanilla flavor, use a real vanilla bean.

Ciasteczka Miodowe z Orzechami
Honey-Nut Cookies

SERVES: 25 - 30 COOKIES **PREP TIME: 20 MINS** **BAKING TIME: 12 - 15 MINS**

In Polish tradition, baking with honey symbolizes sweetness, good health, and prosperity. Ciasteczka Miodowe z Orzechami are often made during holidays as wishes for a prosperous and sweet year ahead!

Ingredients

Cookie Dough
- **250g (2 cups)** all-purpose flour
- **100g (7 tbsp)** unsalted butter, softened
- **100g (½ cup)** granulated sugar
- **100g (¾ cup)** finely ground nuts
- **3 tbsp** honey
- **1 large** egg
- **1 tsp** vanilla extract
- **1 tsp** baking powder
- **Pinch** of salt

Decoration (Optional)
- Whole or chopped nuts for decoration
- Powdered sugar for dusting

Instructions

Prepare the Dough
- In a bowl, cream together butter and sugar until fluffy.
- Add egg, honey, and vanilla extract, mixing thoroughly.
- Gradually add in flour, baking powder, ground nuts, and salt until combined into a soft dough.
- Wrap dough in plastic wrap and refrigerate for 30 minutes.

Shape and Bake Cookies
- Preheat oven to 180°C (350°F). Line baking trays with parchment paper.
- Roll dough into walnut-sized balls and flatten gently.
- Decorate each cookie by lightly pressing a whole nut or chopped nuts onto the surface.
- Bake for 12–15 minutes until golden brown.
- Cool cookies on a wire rack.

Decorate and Serve
- Dust lightly with powdered sugar.
- Ground chocolate

Storage Tips
- Store cookies in an airtight container at room temperature for up to 1 week.
- Cookies taste better after resting a day, as flavors intensify.

Chapter Three

Pastries & Breads
(Wypieki i Pieczywo)

Rogaliki

Traditional Polish Crescent Cookies

SERVES: 24 COOKIES   **PREP TIME: 30 MINS + 1 HOUR RESTING TIME**   **BAKING TIME: 15 - 18 MINS**

In Polish tradition, crescent-shaped cookies (Rogaliki) symbolize good fortune and abundance, making them popular treats served at celebrations to bring luck and prosperity into homes!

Ingredients

Cookie Dough
- **250g (2 cups)** all-purpose flour
- **200g (14 tbsp)** unsalted butter, cold
- **100g (½ cup)** granulated sugar
- **100g (½ cup)** cream cheese or Polish twaróg, softened (optional, makes dough tender)
- **1 large** egg yolk
- **1 tsp** vanilla extract
- **Pinch** of salt

Filling
- Fruit jam (plum, raspberry, apricot)
- Chocolate spread (Nutella)
- Poppy seed filling
- Chopped nuts mixed with sugar

Decoration
- Powdered sugar for dusting

Instructions

Prepare the Dough
- In a bowl, combine flour, softened butter, sugar, egg yolk, vanilla extract, and salt. Knead gently until a smooth dough forms.
- Wrap dough in plastic wrap and chill for about 1 hour to firm.

Shape the Rogaliki
- Preheat oven to **180°C (350°F)**. Line baking trays with parchment paper.
- Divide dough into **two portions**, roll each portion into a round shape (about 3 mm / ⅛-inch thick).
- Cut each dough circle into 8–12 equal triangle-shaped wedges.
- Add **½ teaspoon filling** to the wide edge of each triangle.
- Roll from the wide side toward the tip, shaping them into crescents.

Bake the Rogaliki
- Place shaped crescent cookies on prepared trays, spacing about 3 cm apart.
- Bake for 15–18 minutes until golden around the edges.
- Let cool on trays for a few minutes, then transfer to wire racks.

Decorate and Serve
- Dust generously with powdered sugar before serving.

Storage Tips
- Store cookies airtight at room temperature up to 1 week.
- Experiment with various fillings to discover your favorite combinations.

Rogale Marcińskie
Polish St. Martin's Croissants

SERVES: 12 CROISSANTS **PREP TIME: 2 - 3 HOURS INCL RESTING** **BAKING TIME: 20 - 25 MINS**

In Poznań, Poland, only bakeries officially certified by the city can use the name "Rogale Marcińskie," making these delicious pastries officially protected and beloved symbols of local culinary heritage!

Ingredients

Dough
- **500 g (4 cups)** all-purpose flour
- **250 ml (1 cup)** warm milk
- **2½ tsp (7 g)** dry yeast (or 25 g fresh yeast)
- **60 g (¼ cup)** granulated sugar
- **2 large** eggs
- **1 tsp** vanilla extract
- **½ tsp** salt
- **200 g (14 tbsp)** unsalted butter, cold

White Poppy Seed Filling
- **250 g (1½ cups)** white poppy seeds (ground finely)
- **100 g (½ cup)** almonds (finely chopped)
- **100 g (½ cup)** walnuts or hazelnuts (chopped)
- **100 g (½ cup)** raisins or dried fruit (chopped)
- **100 g (½ cup)** honey
- • **2 tbsp** butter
- • **1 tsp** almond extract
- • **Zest of 1** orange
- • **1 egg white** (beaten lightly, to bind)

Icing and Decoration
- **150 g (1 cup)** powdered sugar
- **2–3 tbsp** milk or lemon juice
- Chopped almonds or walnuts for sprinkling

Instructions

Prepare the Dough
- In a bowl, mix warm milk, yeast, and 1 tsp sugar; let it activate (10 mins).
- In another bowl, combine flour, remaining sugar, salt, eggs, vanilla extract, and activated yeast mixture. Knead into a smooth dough (about 10 mins).
- Wrap dough in plastic wrap and chill for 1 hour.
- Roll dough into a rectangle. Place thinly sliced cold butter onto the dough, fold, and roll several times (similar to puff pastry). Refrigerate between folds for 30 mins. Repeat folding at least 3 times, refrigerating each time.

Prepare Filling
- Rinse and soak white poppy seeds in boiling water for 20 mins. Drain well and grind finely.
- In a saucepan, heat butter, add poppy seeds, almonds, walnuts, raisins, honey, almond extract, and orange zest. Stir over low heat for 5 mins.
- Cool slightly, then stir in beaten egg white.

Shape Croissants
- Preheat oven to 180°C (350°F). Line trays with parchment paper.
- Roll dough out into rectangles, then cut triangles (approx. 12 cm base width).
- Spread filling generously over each triangle, then roll from wide end to tip, forming crescents.

Bake Rogale Marcinskie
- Place croissants onto prepared trays.
- Bake for 20–25 mins until golden brown.
- Cool on wire racks.

Decorate and Serve
- Combine powdered sugar with milk/lemon juice to create icing; drizzle generously.
- Sprinkle with chopped almonds or walnuts.

Storage Tips
- Best eaten within 2 days; store at room temperature, covered lightly.
- Dough can be made in advance and refrigerated overnight before shaping and baking.

Kołacz
Traditional Polish Sweet Bread

SERVES: 10 - 12 SLICES   **PREP TIME: 30 MINS + 2 HOURS RISING TIME**   **BAKING TIME: 35 - 40 MINS**

In Polish tradition, Kołacz is frequently baked for weddings and celebrations to symbolize prosperity and abundance. Guests often share slices, believing it brings good luck and happiness!

Ingredients

Dough
- **500 g (4 cups)** all-purpose flour
- **250 ml (1 cup)** warm milk
- **100 g (½ cup)** granulated sugar
- **7 g (2½ tsp)** dry yeast (or 25 g fresh yeast)
- **100 g (7 tbsp)** unsalted butter, soft
- **2 large** eggs
- **1 tsp** vanilla extract
- **Pinch** of salt

Fillings (Optional)
- Fruit jam, sweet cheese (twaróg), poppy seed filling, or fruit slices

Streusel Topping (Kruszonka)
- **100 g (¾ cup)** flour
- **50 g (¼ cup)** granulated sugar
- **60 g (4 tbsp)** cold butter

Instructions

Prepare the Dough
- In a bowl, combine warm milk, yeast, and 1 tbsp sugar. Set aside 10 minutes until frothy.
- In a separate bowl, mix flour, remaining sugar, salt, eggs, vanilla, and yeast mixture. Knead lightly.
- Gradually add softened butter, kneading into a smooth dough (10 mins).
- Cover dough and let rise in a warm place until doubled (~1½ hours).

Prepare Streusel (Kruszonka)
- Combine flour, sugar, and cold butter using fingertips, forming small crumbles. Refrigerate until needed.

Shape
- Preheat oven to 180°C (350°F). Line baking pan with parchment paper.
- Roll dough into a circle or oval, approximately 2 cm (¾-inch) thick.
- Transfer dough to baking pan. If adding filling, spread gently in the center, leaving a border.

Top and Bake
- Sprinkle generously with prepared streusel topping (kruszonka).
- Let rest again briefly (15 mins).
- Bake at **180°C (350°F)** for **35–40 mins** until golden and cooked through.
- Cool slightly before slicing.

Storage Tips
- Store bread airtight at room temperature up to 1 week.
- Experiment with various fillings to discover your favorite combinations.

Drożdżówki

Traditional Polish Sweet Yeast Rolls

SERVES: 12 - 15 ROLLS **PREP TIME: 30 MINS + 1.5 HOURS RISING TIME** **BAKING TIME: 20 - 25 MINS**

In Poland, freshly-baked Drożdżówki are popular street-food snacks, frequently purchased by students and commuters for a quick breakfast or afternoon treat from local bakeries.

Ingredients

Dough
- **500g (4 cups)** all-purpose flour
- **250 ml (1 cup)** warm milk
- **100g (½ cup)** granulated sugar
- **7 g (2½ tsp)** active dry yeast
- **100g (7 tbsp)** unsalted butter, softened
- **2 large** eggs
- **1 tsp** vanilla extract
- **½ tsp** salt

Fillings (Optional)
- Fruit jam (plum, raspberry, cherry)
- Sweet cheese filling (farmer's cheese mixed with sugar & vanilla)
- Chocolate spread (Nutella)
- Poppy seed filling

Egg Wash
- **1 egg**, lightly beaten

Instructions

Prepare the Dough
- Mix warm milk, yeast, and 1 tbsp sugar; let rest for 10 minutes until bubbly.
- Combine remaining sugar, flour, and salt separately.
- Add yeast mixture, beaten egg, and melted butter to dry ingredients; knead until smooth and elastic.
- Let dough rise, covered, in a warm place for 1 hour until doubled.

Shape Drożdżówki
- Divide dough into equal portions, roll each into flat circles.
- Place 1 tbsp filling of your choice in the center of each circle.
- Fold edges to seal or shape into spirals or crescent rolls.
- Place on parchment-lined baking trays and let rise 30 mins.

Bake Rolls
- Preheat oven to 180°C (350°F).
- Brush rolls gently with beaten egg wash.
- Bake for 20–25 minutes until golden and puffed.
- Cool slightly before serving.

Storage Tips
- Store at room temperature, in an airtight container for up to 2–3 days.
- Reheat briefly before serving for freshness.

Chałka
Traditional Polish Sweet Braided Bread

SERVES: 12 - 14 SLICES **PREP TIME: 30 MINS + 2 HOURS RISING TIME** **BAKING TIME: 30 - 35 MINS**

In Poland, Chałka is traditionally enjoyed during Sunday breakfasts and festive holidays, symbolizing unity, warmth, and family togetherness. It's especially common during celebrations like Christmas and Easter, representing abundance and family closeness.

Ingredients

Dough
- **500g (4 cups)** all-purpose flour
- **250ml (1 cup)** warm milk
- **7g (2¼ tsp)** dry yeast (or 25g fresh yeast)
- **100g (½ cup)** granulated sugar
- **80g (5½ tbsp)** unsalted butter, melted
- **2 large** eggs
- **1 tsp** vanilla extract
- **½ tsp** salt

Egg Wash
- **1 egg**, lightly beaten
- **1 tbsp** milk

Decoration
- Poppy seeds or sesame seeds (traditional topping)

Instructions

Prepare the Dough
- Mix warm milk, yeast, and 1 tbsp sugar in a bowl. Let stand for 10 mins until frothy.
- In a large bowl, combine flour, remaining sugar, yeast mixture, and lightly beaten eggs.
- Knead dough by hand or mixer for 10 mins, adding softened butter gradually. Knead until smooth and elastic.
- Cover dough and let rise in a warm place for about 1½ hours until doubled in size.

Shape the Loaf
- Punch down risen dough. Divide into three equal portions.
- Roll each portion into a long rope, about **40 cm (16 inches)** long.
- Join ropes at one end and braid into a neat, even loaf. Pinch ends to seal.

Second Rise and Baking
- Place braided loaf on parchment-lined baking tray. Cover and let rise for 30 minutes.
- Preheat oven to 180°C (350°F).
- Brush top lightly with beaten egg wash; sprinkle with poppy seeds or almonds, if desired.
- Bake for 30–35 mins until golden brown and cooked through.
- Cool and serve.

Storage Tips
- Store wrapped airtight at room temperature up to 3 days.
- Chałka also freezes very well for up to 2 months.

Buchtelki
Polish Sweet Yeast Rolls

SERVES: 12 - 15 ROLLS **PREP TIME: 25 MINS + 2 HOURS RISING TIME** **BAKING TIME: 25 - 30 MINS**

Although popular across Poland, Buchtelki originated from the region of Silesia, strongly influenced by Austrian culinary traditions. They became a favorite comfort food in Poland, often served as Sunday breakfast treats or special desserts during festive occasions!

Ingredients

Dough
- **500g (4 cups)** all-purpose flour
- **250 ml (1 cup)** warm milk
- **7 g (2¼ tsp)** active dry yeast (or 25 g fresh yeast)
- **100 g (½ cup)** sugar
- **100 g (7 tbsp)** unsalted butter, soft
- **2 large** eggs
- **1 tsp** vanilla extract
- **Pinch** of salt

Filling Options
- Fruit jam (plum, raspberry, apricot)
- Sweet farmer's cheese filling (twaróg with sugar & vanilla)
- Chocolate spread or Nutella

Topping
- Powdered sugar (for dusting)
- Melted butter (optional, for brushing)

Instructions

Prepare the Dough
- Mix warm milk, yeast, and 1 tbsp sugar. Let sit for 10 minutes until frothy.
- In a bowl, combine flour, remaining sugar, yeast mixture, softened butter, eggs, and vanilla. Knead dough for 10 minutes until smooth and elastic.
- Cover dough with a towel; let rise for 1 hour in a warm place until doubled.

Shape Buchtelki
- Divide dough into 12–15 portions. Flatten each into a small circle.
- Place 1 teaspoon of filling (jam or sweet cheese) in the center of each.
- Pinch edges firmly to seal, shaping into round balls.

Second Rise and Baking
- Arrange rolls seam-side down in a greased baking dish, close together.
- Cover lightly, let rise again for 30 minutes.
- Preheat oven to 180°C (350°F).
- Optional: Brush tops with melted butter for extra golden crust.
- Bake for 25-30 mins until golden and puffed.
- Cool and serve.

Storage Tips
- Best enjoyed fresh. Store leftovers airtight for up to 2–3 days.
- Reheat gently before serving to refresh softness.

Jagodzianki
Polish Blueberry-Filled Sweet Rolls

SERVES: 12 ROLLS   **PREP TIME:** 30 MINS + 1.5 HOURS RISING TIME   **BAKING TIME:** 20 - 25 MINS

In Poland, freshly baked Jagodzianki are considered an iconic symbol of summertime, particularly popular in northern Poland and the Masuria region, where wild blueberries (jagody) grow abundantly in the forests!

Ingredients

Dough
- 500g (4 cups) all-purpose flour
- 250ml (1 cup) warm milk
- 7g (2¼ tsp) active dry yeast (or 25g fresh yeast)
- 100g (½ cup) sugar
- 80g (5½ tbsp) unsalted butter, soft
- 2 large eggs
- 1 tsp vanilla extract
- Pinch of salt

Filling
- 300g (2 cups) fresh blueberries
- 50g (¼ cup) sugar
- 1 tbsp cornstarch (optional, helps thicken juices)

Glaze (Optional)
- 120g (1 cup) powdered sugar
- 2 tbsp lemon juice or milk

Egg Wash
- 1 egg, lightly beaten

Instructions

Prepare the Dough
- Combine warm milk, yeast, and 1 tbsp sugar. Let rest 10 mins until frothy.
- Mix flour, remaining sugar, salt, eggs, vanilla, yeast mixture, and softened butter. Knead into smooth dough (~10 mins).
- Cover dough, let rise in warm place for 1 hour until doubled.

Prepare Blueberry Filling
- Gently mix fresh blueberries, sugar, and cornstarch. Set aside.

Shape the Jagodzianki
- Divide dough into 12 portions. Flatten each piece into a circle (~10 cm/4 inches diameter).
- Place 1–2 tablespoons blueberry filling in center. Pinch edges securely closed.
- Place rolls seam-side down on baking trays lined with parchment paper. Let rise for another 30 mins.

Bake
- Preheat oven to 180°C (350°F).
- Brush rolls gently with beaten egg.
- Bake 20–25 mins until golden brown.
- Allow to cool slightly.

Glaze and Serve
- Mix powdered sugar with lemon juice or milk; drizzle over warm rolls.
- Serve warm or at room temperature.

Storage Tips
- Store rolls in an airtight container at room temperature for 2–3 days.
- Best enjoyed freshly baked or reheated gently before serving.

Bułeczki z Makiem
Polish Poppy Seed Sweet Buns

SERVES: 12 BUNS   **PREP TIME: 30 MINS + 1.5 HOURS RISING TIME**   **BAKING TIME: 20 - 25 MINS**

In Poland, pastries with poppy seeds symbolize abundance, prosperity, and good fortune. Serving Drożdżówki z Makiem during celebrations, especially at Christmas and New Year, is a way to wish family and friends prosperity for the coming year!

Ingredients

Dough
- **500 g (4 cups)** all-purpose flour
- **250 ml (1 cup)** warm milk
- **7 g (2¼ tsp)** active dry yeast (or 25 g fresh yeast)
- **100 g (½ cup)** granulated sugar
- **100 g (7 tbsp)** unsalted butter, soft
- **2 large** eggs
- **1 tsp** vanilla extract
- **½ tsp** salt

Poppy Seed Filling
- **250 g (2 cups)** ground poppy seeds (pre-soaked, boiled, and ground, or canned)
- **100 g (½ cup)** sugar or honey
- **50 g (3½ tbsp)** unsalted butter
- **50 g (⅓ cup)** raisins (optional)
- **1 tsp** almond extract or vanilla extract
- **1 tsp** lemon zest (optional)

Egg Wash
- **1 egg**, lightly beaten

Glaze (Optional)
- **120 g (1 cup)** powdered sugar
- **2 tbsp** milk or lemon juice

Instructions

Prepare the Dough
- In a bowl, mix warm milk, yeast, and 1 tsp sugar; let activate (10 minutes).
- Combine flour, remaining sugar, salt, eggs, vanilla, and yeast mixture. Knead gently (10 mins), gradually adding softened butter, until dough is smooth.
- Cover dough, let rise (1 hour) until doubled.

Prepare Filling
- In a saucepan, mix ground poppy seeds, sugar/honey, vanilla, and a tablespoon of butter, stirring until thickened (5–10 mins). Cool slightly before use.

Shape the Buns
- Divide dough into 12 equal parts.
- Flatten each portion slightly, add a tablespoon of filling in the center, and seal dough around filling, forming round buns.
- Place buns seam-side down on parchment-lined trays, spaced about 4 cm apart. Let rise 30 minutes.

Bake Buns
- Preheat oven to 180°C (350°F).
- Brush tops with beaten egg wash or melted butter.
- Bake 20–25 mins until golden brown.
- Cool on wire racks.

Decorate and Serve
- Drizzle lightly with glaze made from powdered sugar and milk (optional).
- Serve warm or at room temperature with tea or coffee.

Storage Tips
- Store buns covered at room temperature up to 3 days.
- Reheat briefly before serving to enhance texture and aroma.

Bułeczki Cynamonowe
Polish Cinnamon Buns

SERVES: 12 BUNS **PREP TIME: 30 MINS + 1.5 HOURS RISING TIME** **BAKING TIME: 20 - 25 MINS**

In Poland, the aroma of freshly baked cinnamon buns (Bułeczki Cynamonowe) is closely associated with cozy family gatherings, particularly enjoyed during colder months, as cinnamon's warming scent is believed to bring comfort and happiness!

Ingredients

Dough
- **500 g (4 cups)** all-purpose flour
- **250 ml (1 cup)** warm milk
- **7 g (2¼ tsp)** active dry yeast (or 25 g fresh yeast)
- **100 g (½ cup)** granulated sugar
- **80 g (5.5 tbsp)** unsalted butter, soft
- **2 large** eggs
- **1 tsp** vanilla extract
- **½ tsp** salt

Cinnamon Filling
- **100 g (½ cup)** brown sugar
- **2 tbsp** ground cinnamon
- **80 g (5½ tbsp)** unsalted butter, softened

Egg Wash
- **1 egg**, lightly beaten

Icing (Optional)
- **150 g (1¼ cups)** powdered sugar
- **2 tbsp** milk or cream
- **½ tsp** vanilla extract

Instructions

Prepare the Dough
- Combine warm milk, yeast, and 1 tbsp sugar; rest 10 mins until frothy.
- In a bowl, mix flour, remaining sugar, salt, eggs, vanilla, yeast mixture, and softened butter. Knead for 10 mins until smooth.
- Cover dough and rise in a warm place (1 hour) until doubled.

Prepare Cinnamon Filling
- Mix softened butter, brown sugar, and cinnamon until creamy and spreadable.

Shape Cinnamon Buns
- Roll dough into a rectangle (40x25 cm /16x10 inches), spread cinnamon filling evenly.
- Roll dough tightly into a long log; cut into 12 equal pieces.
- Place buns into greased baking pan, spacing evenly. Let rise another 30 mins.

Bake Buns
- Preheat oven to 180°C (350°F).
- Brush tops gently with beaten egg.
- Bake for 20–25 mins until golden brown.
4. Cool briefly.

Glaze and Serve
- Drizzle warm buns with icing made by mixing powdered sugar, milk, and vanilla.
- Serve warm or at room temperature.

Storage Tips
- Store buns covered at room temperature for up to 2–3 days.
- Reheat briefly for best taste.

Kołaczki

Traditional Polish Filled Pastries

SERVES: 24 PASTRIES **PREP TIME: 25 MINS + 1 HOUR CHILLING TIME** **BAKING TIME: 12 - 15 MINS**

In Polish tradition, baking Kołaczki is often a family activity, with generations gathering together during holidays to prepare these pastries, symbolizing family unity, warmth, and hospitality!

Ingredients

Dough
- **250g (2 cups)** all-purpose flour
- **200g (7 oz)** cream cheese, softened
- **200g (14 tbsp)** unsalted butter, softened
- **50g (¼ cup)** sugar
- **1 tsp** vanilla extract
- **Pinch** of salt

Filling Options
- Fruit jam (raspberry, apricot, plum, strawberry)
- Sweet cheese filling (twaróg mixed with sugar & vanilla)
- Poppy seed filling (masa makowa)
- Nut filling (ground walnuts, sugar, and honey)

Topping
- Powdered sugar for dusting

Instructions

Prepare the Dough
- Cream softened butter and cream cheese until smooth and creamy.
- Add sugar, vanilla extract, salt, and flour; mix gently into a smooth dough.
- Wrap dough in plastic wrap and chill for at least 1 hour in the fridge.

Shape the Pastries
- Preheat oven to 180°C (350°F). Line baking sheets with parchment paper.
- Roll chilled dough thinly (3–4 mm/⅛-inch thick) on a floured surface.
- Cut into small squares (approximately 6–7 cm / 2½ inches wide).
- Place 1 teaspoon filling in the center of each square.
- Fold opposite corners together, pinching gently to seal.

Bake Pastries
- Place pastries on lined baking sheets, spacing about 3 cm apart.
- Bake at 180°C (350°F) for 12–15 minutes until lightly golden.
- Allow pastries to cool completely on wire racks.

Serve
- Dust generously with powdered sugar.
- Serve pastries at room temperature.

Storage Tips
- Store Kołaczki in an airtight container at room temperature for up to 1 week.
- Pastries freeze well for up to 2 months.

Kiełbasa z Makiem
Polish Poppy Seed-Stuffed Sweet Roll

SERVES: 10 - 12 SLICES **PREP TIME:** 40 MINS + 2 HOUR RISING TIME **BAKING TIME:** 30 - 35 MINS

In Polish tradition, eating poppy seed-filled desserts like Kiełbasa z Makiem during Christmas Eve (Wigilia) is believed to bring good luck, prosperity, and abundance in the coming year! And despite its name, it is not an actual sausage but rather a sweet treat that will have you wanting more.

Ingredients

Dough
- **500g (4 cups)** all-purpose flour
- **250ml (1 cup)** warm milk
- **7g (2¼ tsp)** active dry yeast (or 25g fresh yeast)
- **100g (½ cup)** granulated sugar
- **80g (5½ tbsp)** unsalted butter, soft
- **2 large** eggs
- **1 tsp** vanilla extract
- **½ tsp** salt

Poppy Seed Filling
- 250g (2 cups) ground poppy seeds (pre-soaked and ground, or canned poppy seed filling)
- 100g (½ cup) sugar or honey
- 50g (3½ tbsp) unsalted butter
- 50g (⅓ cup) chopped walnuts (optional)
- 50g (⅓ cup) raisins (optional)
- 1 tsp vanilla extract
- **1 tsp** lemon zest (optional)
- **1 egg white**, lightly beaten (to bind the filling)

Egg Wash
- **1 egg yolk** + **1 tbsp** milk

Optional Glaze
- **120g (1 cup)** powdered sugar
- **2 tbsp** milk or lemon juice

Instructions

Prepare the Dough
- In a bowl, mix warm milk, yeast, and 1 tbsp sugar; let rest 10 minutes until frothy.
- In a large bowl, combine flour, remaining sugar, salt, eggs, vanilla, yeast mixture, and knead gently (10 mins).
- Gradually add softened butter and knead until smooth.
- Cover dough and let rise in a warm place for 1 hour until doubled.

Prepare the Poppy Seed Filling
- If using whole poppy seeds, soak in boiling water for 20 minutes, drain well, and grind finely.
- In a saucepan, melt butter, then add poppy seeds, sugar (or honey), walnuts, raisins, almond extract, and lemon zest. Stir over low heat for 5–10 minutes.
- Remove from heat, let cool, then mix in lightly beaten egg white to help bind the filling.

Shape the Roll
- Roll out the dough into a 30x40 cm (12x16 inch) rectangle.
- Spread the poppy seed filling evenly over the dough, leaving 1 cm (½ inch) border.
- Roll tightly from the longer side to form a log (like a sausage). Seal the edges well.

Second Rise and Baking
- Place roll on a parchment-lined baking tray, seam-side down. Cover and let rise again for **30 minutes**.
- Preheat oven to **180°C (350°F)**.
- Brush with egg wash and bake for **30–35 minutes** until golden brown.

Glaze and Serve
- If using glaze, mix powdered sugar with milk or lemon juice and drizzle over cooled roll.
- Slice and serve at room temperature.

Storage Tips
- Store in an airtight container at room temperature for up to 3 days.
- The roll can be frozen for up to 2 months—thaw at room temperature before serving.

Kukurydziane Ciasteczka
Polish Corn Cookies

SERVES: 24 COOKIES **PREP TIME: 15 MINS** **BAKING TIME: 12 - 15 MINS** **RESTING TIME: 15 MINS**

Corn-based cookies have been a part of Polish rural cuisine for centuries, as cornmeal was widely used in villages where wheat flour was scarce. Over time, these cookies became a nostalgic treat, especially loved in southern Poland!

Ingredients

Dough
- **200g (1½ cups)** all-purpose flour
- **100g (¾ cup)** cornmeal (or cornstarch for a softer version)
- **120g (½ cup)** granulated sugar
- **150g (10½ tbsp)** unsalted butter, soft
- **2 large** egg yolks
- **1 tsp** vanilla extract
- **½ tsp** baking powder
- **Pinch** of salt

Optional Toppings
- Powdered sugar (for dusting)
- Melted chocolate (for drizzling)

Instructions

Prepare the Dough
- Preheat oven to 180°C (350°F) and line a baking sheet with parchment paper.
- In a large bowl, cream together butter and sugar until light and fluffy.
- Add egg yolks and vanilla extract, mixing until well combined.
- In a separate bowl, mix flour, cornmeal (or cornstarch), baking powder, and salt.
- Gradually add dry ingredients to the butter mixture, stirring until a soft dough forms.

Shape the Cookies
- Roll dough into small balls (about **2 cm in diameter**).
- Place them on the baking sheet, spacing about **3 cm apart**.
- Flatten each ball slightly with your fingers or a fork.

Bake the Cookies
- Bake for 12–15 minutes, until the edges turn lightly golden.
- Let cool on a wire rack.

Decorate and Serve
- Dust with **powdered sugar** or drizzle with **melted chocolate** (optional).

Storage Tips
- Store in an airtight container at room temperature for up to 1 week.
- For a citrusy twist, add lemon zest to the dough.

Marcepanowy Rogalik
Polish Marzipan Crescent Rolls

SERVES: 12 CRESCENT ROLLS   **PREP TIME:** 30 MINS + 1 HOUR RISING   **BAKING TIME:** 18 - 22 MINS

Marzipan has been a luxury ingredient in Poland for centuries, originally imported from the Middle East. Polish bakers incorporated it into crescent rolls, creating this rich and elegant pastry, often served at royal and noble feasts!

Ingredients

Dough
- **250g (2 cups)** all-purpose flour
- **125ml (½ cup)** warm milk
- **5g (1½ tsp)** dry yeast (or 15g fresh yeast)
- **50g (¼ cup)** granulated sugar
- **75g (5 tbsp)** unsalted butter, softened
- **1 large** egg
- **1 tsp** vanilla extract
- **Pinch** of salt

For the Marzipan Filling
- **150g (5 oz)** marzipan paste
- **50g (¼ cup)** powdered sugar
- **1** egg white
- **½ tsp** almond extract (optional)

For the Egg Wash
- **1 egg yolk + 1 tbsp** milk (for brushing before baking)

For Decoration
- Powdered sugar (for dusting)
- Sliced almonds (optional)

Instructions

Prepare the Dough
- In a small bowl, mix warm milk, yeast, and 1 tbsp sugar. Let sit for 10 minutes until frothy.
- In a large bowl, mix flour, remaining sugar, salt, softened butter, egg, vanilla extract, and yeast mixture.
- Knead into a soft, smooth dough (10 minutes).
- Cover and let rise in a warm place for 1 hour until doubled.

Prepare the Marzipan Filling
- In a bowl, mix marzipan paste, powdered sugar, egg white, and almond extract into a smooth filling.
- Roll filling into small logs (~6 cm / 2½ inches long) for each crescent.

Shape the Crescent Rolls
- Roll dough into a 30 cm (12-inch) circle on a floured surface.
- Cut into 12 equal triangular wedges.
- Place a marzipan log at the base of each triangle.
- Roll from the wide end toward the point, forming crescents and place seam-side down.

Second Rise and Baking
- Let crescents rise 30 minutes while preheating the oven to 180°C (350°F).
- Brush tops with egg wash.
- Bake for 18–22 minutes until golden brown.
- Cool on a wire rack.

Decorate and Serve
- Dust with powdered sugar before serving.
- Sprinkle with sliced almonds for extra crunch (optional).

Storage Tips
- Store at room temperature in an airtight container for 2–3 days.
- For extra flavor, add orange zest to the marzipan filling.

Babka Wielkanocna
Traditional Polish Easter Cake

SERVES: 10 - 12 SLICES **PREP TIME:** 30 MINS + 1.5 HOUR RISING **BAKING TIME:** 40 - 45 MINS

In Polish Easter tradition, Babka is often blessed in a church along with other festive foods in the Święconka basket, symbolizing prosperity and divine blessings for the year ahead!

Ingredients

Dough
- **500g (4 cups)** all-purpose flour
- **250ml (1 cup)** warm milk
- **7g (2¼ tsp)** active dry yeast
- **100g (½ cup)** granulated sugar
- **80g (5½ tbsp)** unsalted butter, melted
- **3 large** eggs
- **1 tsp** vanilla extract
- **1 tbsp** rum or lemon juice (optional)
- **Zest of 1** lemon or orange
- **½ tsp** salt

For the Egg Wash
- **1 egg** yolk + **1 tbsp** milk

For Decoration
- **Powdered sugar** (for dusting)
- **Glaze: 120g (1 cup)** powdered sugar + **2 tbsp** lemon juice or milk

Instructions

Prepare the Dough
- In a small bowl, combine warm milk, yeast, and 1 tbsp sugar. Let sit for 10 minutes until frothy.
- In a large bowl, whisk together flour, remaining sugar, salt, and citrus zest.
- Add yeast mixture, eggs, vanilla extract, and rum (if using). Mix well.
- Gradually incorporate melted butter, kneading for 10–15 minutes until smooth.
- Cover dough with a clean towel and let rise for 1½ hours until doubled in size.

Shape and Second Rise
- Grease a **bundt pan or tall cake pan** with butter.
- Transfer dough to the pan and smooth the top.
- Cover and let rise again for **30 minutes**.

Bake the Babka
- Preheat oven to 180°C (350°F).
- Brush the top with egg wash.
- Bake for 40–45 minutes until golden brown.
- Allow to cool in the pan for 10 minutes, then transfer to a wire rack.

Decorate and Serve
- Dust with **powdered sugar** OR
- Drizzle with **glaze** (mix powdered sugar with lemon juice or milk).

Storage Tips
- Store in an airtight container for 3 days at room temperature.
- Babka can be frozen for up to 1 month.

Babka Marmurkowa
Polish Marble Cake

SERVES: 10 - 12 SLICES **PREP TIME: 20 MINS** **BAKING TIME: 45 - 50 MINS** **RESTING TIME: 1 HOUR**

The word "babka" means "grandmother" in Polish, and the cake's shape resembles the long, pleated skirts traditionally worn by grandmothers in Poland!

Ingredients

For the Batter
- **250g (2 cups)** all-purpose flour
- **200g (1 cup)** granulated sugar
- **150g (10 tbsp)** unsalted butter, softened
- **4 large** eggs
- **125ml (½ cup)** milk
- **2 tsp** baking powder
- **1 tsp** vanilla extract
- **Pinch** of salt

For the Chocolate Swirl
- **2 tbsp** unsweetened cocoa powder
- **2 tbsp** milk
- **1 tbsp** sugar (optional)

For Decoration
- Powdered sugar for dusting OR
- Chocolate glaze **(100g melted dark chocolate + 1 tbsp butter)**

Instructions

Prepare the Batter
- Preheat oven to 180°C (350°F). Grease and flour a bundt or loaf pan.
- In a bowl, cream butter and sugar until light.
- Add eggs one at a time, mixing well.
- Stir in vanilla extract.
- Sift together flour, baking powder, and salt, then gradually add to the wet mixture, alternating with milk. Mix until smooth.

Make the Marble Swirl
- In a separate bowl, mix **cocoa powder, sugar (if using), and milk** until smooth.
- Divide the batter into **two equal portions**. Stir the cocoa mixture into one half of the batter.

Assemble the Marble Effect
- Pour **half of the vanilla batter** into the pan.
- Add the **chocolate batter** on top, then finish with the remaining vanilla batter.
- Use a skewer or knife to swirl the batters together for a marbled effect.

Bake the Babka
- Bake for 45–50 minutes, or until a toothpick inserted comes out clean.
- Let the cake cool in the pan for 10 minutes, then transfer to a wire rack.

Decorate and Serve
- Dust with **powdered sugar** OR
- Drizzle with **chocolate glaze** for extra richness.

Storage Tips
- Store at room temperature in an airtight container for 3-4 days.
- Freezes well for up to 1 month (wrap tightly in plastic wrap).

Babka Cytrynowa
Polish Lemon Cake

SERVES: 10 - 12 SLICES **PREP TIME: 20 MINS** **BAKING TIME: 45 - 50 MINS** **RESTING TIME: 1 HOUR**

In Poland, Babka Cytrynowa is a traditional Easter dessert, symbolizing the arrival of spring and new beginnings. The lemon flavor represents freshness and renewal, making it a perfect treat for celebrating Easter Sunday!

Ingredients

For the Batter
- **250g (2 cups)** all-purpose flour
- **200g (1 cup)** granulated sugar
- **150g (10 tbsp)** unsalted butter, soft
- **4 large** eggs
- **125ml (½ cup)** milk
- **2 tsp** baking powder
- **1 tsp** vanilla extract
- Zest and juice of **1 large** lemon
- **Pinch** of salt

For the Lemon Glaze
- **150g (1¼ cups)** powdered sugar
- **2–3 tbsp** fresh lemon juice

Instructions

Prepare the Dough
- Preheat oven to 180°C (350°F). Grease and flour a bundt or loaf pan.
- In a bowl, cream together butter and sugar until light and fluffy.
- Add eggs one at a time, beating well after each addition.
- Stir in vanilla extract, lemon zest, and lemon juice.
- Sift together flour, baking powder, and salt, then gradually add to the wet mixture, alternating with milk. Mix until smooth.

Bake the Babka
- Pour batter into the prepared pan and smooth the top.
- Bake for **45–50 minutes**, or until a toothpick inserted in the center comes out clean.
- Let the cake cool in the pan for **10 minutes**, then transfer to a wire rack to cool completely.

Prepare the Lemon Glaze
- In a small bowl, whisk together powdered sugar and lemon juice until smooth.
- Drizzle over the cooled babka and let it set.

Serve
- Optionally, dust with powdered sugar instead of using the glaze.

Storage Tips
- Store in an airtight container at room temperature for 3–4 days.
- Can be frozen for up to 1 month (wrap tightly in plastic wrap).
- For extra flavor, add 1 tbsp of limoncello or rum to the batter.

Babka Czekoladowa
Polish Chocolate Cake

SERVES: 10 - 12 SLICES | **PREP TIME:** 20 MINS | **BAKING TIME:** 45 - 50 MINS | **RESTING TIME:** 1 HOUR

In Poland, Babka is traditionally associated with Easter, symbolizing abundance and family unity. The chocolate version, Babka Czekoladowa, became popular in the 20th century as chocolate became more widely available, making it a favorite among children and adults alike!

Ingredients

For the Batter
- **250g (2 cups)** all-purpose flour
- **200g (1 cup)** granulated sugar
- **150g (10 tbsp)** unsalted butter, soft
- **4 large** eggs
- **125ml (½ cup)** milk
- **2 tsp** baking powder
- **½ tsp** baking soda
- **3 tbsp** unsweetened cocoa powder
- **100g (3.5 oz)** dark chocolate, melted
- **1 tsp** vanilla extract

For the Chocolate Glaze
- **100g (3.5 oz)** dark chocolate, melted
- **2 tbsp** butter
- **1 tbsp** milk or cream

For Decoration
- Powdered sugar (for dusting)
- Chopped nuts, chocolate shavings, or sprinkles

Instructions

Prepare the Dough
- Preheat oven to 180°C (350°F). Grease and flour a bundt or loaf pan.
- In a bowl, cream together butter and sugar until light and fluffy.
- Add eggs one at a time, beating well after each addition.
- Stir in vanilla extract and melted dark chocolate.
- Sift together flour, cocoa powder, baking powder, baking soda, and salt.
- Gradually add dry ingredients to the wet mixture, alternating with milk. Mix until smooth.

Bake the Babka
- Pour the batter into the prepared pan and smooth the top.
- Bake for **45–50 minutes**, or until a toothpick inserted in the center comes out clean.
- Let the cake cool in the pan for **10 minutes**, then transfer to a wire rack to cool completely.

Prepare the Chocolate Glaze
- Melt dark chocolate and butter over low heat, stirring until smooth.
- Add milk or cream and mix well.
- Drizzle warm glaze over the cooled babka and let it set.

Serve
- Dust with **powdered sugar** or sprinkle with chocolate shavings.

Storage Tips
- Store in an airtight container at room temperature for 3–4 days.
- Freezes well for up to 1 month (wrap tightly in plastic wrap).
- For a more intense chocolate flavor, use espresso powder in the batter.

Babka Drożdżowa
Polish Yeast Cake

SERVES: 10 - 12 SLICES **PREP TIME: 30 MINS + 2 HOUR RISING TIME** **BAKING TIME: 45 - 50 MINS**

In Polish tradition, Babka Drożdżowa is a must-have for Easter, symbolizing joy, prosperity, and new beginnings. It is often blessed in church on Holy Saturday as part of the Święconka basket, along with bread, eggs, and butter!

Ingredients

For the Yeast Dough
- **500g (4 cups)** all-purpose flour
- **7g (2¼ tsp)** active dry yeast
- **250ml (1 cup)** warm milk
- **100g (½ cup)** granulated sugar
- **100g (7 tbsp)** unsalted butter, melted
- **3 large** eggs
- **1 tsp** vanilla extract
- **Zest of 1** lemon or orange
- **½ tsp** salt
- **50g (⅓ cup)** raisins or dried fruit

For the Egg Wash
- **1 egg** yolk + **1 tbsp** milk

For Decoration
- Powdered sugar (for dusting)
- Glaze: **120g (1 cup)** powdered sugar + **2 tbsp** lemon juice or milk
- Almond slices or chopped nuts

Instructions

Prepare the Yeast Mixture
- In a small bowl, mix warm milk, yeast, and 1 tbsp sugar. Let sit for 10 minutes until frothy.

Prepare the Dough
- In a large bowl, mix flour, remaining sugar, salt, and lemon zest.
- Add yeast mixture, eggs, vanilla extract, and knead the dough for 10 minutes.
- Slowly add melted butter, kneading until fully incorporated and smooth.
- If using raisins, fold them into the dough.
- Cover and let rise in a warm place for 1–1½ hours until doubled in size.

Shape and Second Rise
- Grease a **bundt or tall cake pan** with butter.
- Transfer dough to the pan, smoothing the top.
- Cover and let rise for **30–45 minutes**.

Bake the Babka
- Preheat oven to 180°C (350°F).
- Brush the top with egg wash.
- Bake for 40–45 minutes until golden brown and a toothpick comes out clean.
- Allow to cool in the pan for 10 minutes, then transfer to a wire rack.

Decorate and Serve
- Dust with **powdered sugar** OR
- Drizzle with **glaze** (mix powdered sugar with lemon juice or milk).

Storage Tips
- Store in an airtight container for 3 days at room temperature.
- The dough can be refrigerated overnight for a slower rise.
- To reheat, warm slices in the oven for a few minutes.

Babka Gotowana
Polish Steamed Cake

SERVES: 10 - 12 SLICES   **PREP TIME: 20 MINS**   **STEAMING TIME: 60 - 75 MINS**   **RESTING TIME: 1 HOUR**

The steaming method for Babka Gotowana was traditionally used when ovens were unavailable or unreliable in rural Polish homes. The result? A softer, silkier babka that stays fresher for longer!

Ingredients

For the Yeast Dough
- **250g (2 cups)** all-purpose flour
- **200g (1 cup)** granulated sugar
- **150g (10 tbsp)** unsalted butter, soft
- **4 large** eggs
- **125ml (½ cup)** milk
- **2 tsp** baking powder
- **1 tsp** vanilla extract
- **1 tbsp** rum or lemon juice (optional)
- **Zest of 1** lemon or orange
- **Pinch** of salt

For Decoration
- Powdered sugar (for dusting) **OR**
- **Glaze: 120g (1 cup)** powdered sugar **+ 2 tbsp** lemon juice

Instructions

Prepare the Batter
- In a bowl, cream together butter and sugar until light and fluffy.
- Add eggs one at a time, mixing well after each addition.
- Stir in vanilla extract, rum (if using), and lemon zest.
- In a separate bowl, sift together flour, baking powder, and salt.
- Gradually add dry ingredients to the wet mixture, alternating with milk. Mix until smooth.

Prepare the Steaming Mold
- Grease a **steamed babka mold (with a lid)** or a **tall bundt pan** that can be covered with foil.
- Pour the batter into the mold, leaving **at least 2 cm (¾ inch) space at the top** for expansion.
- Secure the lid or tightly cover the mold with aluminum foil.

Steam the Babka
- Place the mold in a large pot with water reaching halfway up the sides of the mold.
- Cover the pot with a lid and bring water to a gentle boil.
- Steam for 60–75 minutes, ensuring the water level stays consistent (add hot water if needed).
- Test by inserting a toothpick—if it comes out clean, the babka is ready.

Cool and Decorate
- Carefully remove the mold from the pot and let the babka cool for 15 minutes before unmolding.
- Once fully cooled, dust with powdered sugar or drizzle with lemon glaze.

Serve
- Serve warm or at room temperature with tea or coffee.

Storage Tips
- Store at room temperature in an airtight container for 3–4 days.

Babka Piaskowa
Polish Sand Cake

SERVES: 10 - 12 SLICES **PREP TIME: 20 MINS** **BAKING TIME: 45 - 50 MINS** **RESTING TIME: 1 HOUR**

The name "Piaskowa" (meaning sand-like) comes from the cake's fine, dry texture, making it perfect for soaking up coffee or tea. It was a favorite among Polish nobility in the 19th century, often served with fruit preserves!

Ingredients

For the Batter
- **250g (2 cups)** all-purpose flour
- **50g (⅓ cup)** potato starch (for a finer crumb)
- **200g (1 cup)** granulated sugar
- **200g (14 tbsp)** unsalted butter, soft
- **4 large** eggs
- **2 tsp** baking powder
- **½ tsp** vanilla extract
- **Zest of 1** lemon or orange
- **Pinch** of salt

For Decoration
- Powdered sugar (for dusting) **OR**
- **Glaze: 120g (1 cup)** powdered sugar + **2 tbsp** lemon juice

Instructions

Prepare the Batter
- Preheat oven to 180°C (350°F). Grease and flour a bundt or loaf pan.
- In a bowl, cream together butter and sugar until pale and fluffy (about 5 minutes).
- Add eggs one at a time, beating well after each addition.
- Stir in vanilla extract and lemon zest.
- Sift together flour, potato starch, baking powder, and salt.
- Gradually mix dry ingredients into the wet ingredients, stirring until smooth.

Bake the Babka
- Pour batter into the prepared pan, smoothing the top.
- Bake for **45–50 minutes**, or until a toothpick inserted into the center comes out clean.
- Let the babka cool in the pan for **10 minutes**, then transfer to a wire rack.

Decorate and Serve
- Dust with **powdered sugar** OR
- Drizzle with **lemon glaze** for extra flavor.
- Slice and enjoy with tea, coffee, or milk.

Storage Tips
- Store in an airtight container at room temperature for up to 4 days.
- For a more tender crumb, replace potato starch with cornstarch.
- Add cocoa powder to half of the batter for a marble effect.

Mazurek
Traditional Polish Easter Shortcrust Pastry

SERVES: 10 - 12 SLICES   **PREP TIME:** 20 MINS + 30 MINS CHILL TIME   **BAKING TIME:** 15 - 20 MINS

Mazurek is believed to have been inspired by Turkish and Middle Eastern pastries, brought to Poland by traders in the 17th century. It became an Easter staple, symbolizing the end of Lenten fasting and the beginning of feasting!

Ingredients

For the Shortcrust Pastry
- **250g (2 cups)** all-purpose flour
- **150g (10½ tbsp)** cold unsalted butter, cubed
- **50g (¼ cup)** powdered sugar
- **1 egg** yolk
- **2 tbsp** cold water
- **1 tsp** vanilla extract (optional)

For the Toppings (Choose or Mix Multiple Options)
- Fruit jam
- Dulce de leche (kajmak) (sweet caramel spread)
- Melted chocolate (dark or milk)
- Chopped nuts (almonds, walnuts, or hazelnuts)
- Dried fruit
- Powdered sugar or icing (for decoration)

Instructions

Prepare the Pastry Dough
- In a bowl, mix flour and powdered sugar.
- Add cold butter and rub it into the flour with your fingers until it resembles breadcrumbs.
- Add egg yolk, vanilla extract, and cold water, kneading briefly until the dough comes together.
- Wrap in plastic wrap and chill for 30 minutes.

Roll and Bake the Pastry
- Preheat oven to **180°C (350°F)**.
- Roll out the dough into a **rectangular or round shape** (~½ cm thick).
- Transfer to a baking sheet lined with parchment paper. Prick with a fork.
- Bake for **15–20 minutes**, until golden. Let cool completely.

Add Toppings and Decorate
- Spread a layer of fruit jam, dulce de leche (kajmak), or melted chocolate evenly over the cooled pastry.
- Decorate with chopped nuts, dried fruits, or sugar icing in intricate patterns.
- Let the toppings set before slicing.

Serve
- Cut into squares or rectangles and serve at room temperature.

Storage Tips
- Store at room temperature for up to 5 days in an airtight container.
- Get creative with decorations – traditional Easter patterns include crosses, flowers, or lambs made with nuts and icing.
- Try different fillings like orange marmalade for a tangy twist.

Chapter Four

Other Traditional Polish Desserts

Kogel Mogel
Traditional Polish Egg Yolk Dessert

SERVES: 2 **PREP TIME: 5 MINS** **BAKE TIME: 0 MINS** **CHILLING TIME: 20 MINS**

Kogel Mogel inspired the famous song "Kolorowy Wiatr" (Polish version of Colors of the Wind from Pocahontas), in which the singer mentions the dessert in the lyrics! It has also been featured in classic Polish movies and books, making it a nostalgic treat for many generations.

Ingredients

For the Dessert
- **2 fresh egg** yolks (from high-quality eggs)
- **2 tbsp** granulated sugar or honey
- **1 tsp** vanilla extract (optional)

Variations
- **Chocolate version:** Add **1 tsp** cocoa powder
- **Coffee flavor:** Add **½ tsp** instant coffee
- **Alcoholic version:** Add **1 tbsp** rum or advocaat (for adults)

Instructions

Separate the Egg Yolks
- Carefully separate the egg yolks from the whites.
- Place the yolks in a small bowl (ensure there's no egg white).

Whip the Kogel Mogel
- Add **sugar (or honey)** to the yolks.
- Using a whisk or electric mixer, beat until the mixture becomes **pale, thick, and creamy** (about 3–5 minutes).
- If using **vanilla extract, cocoa, or alcohol**, mix it in at the end.

Serve
- Serve immediately in small cups or glasses.

Storage Tips
- Kogel Mogel should be eaten fresh due to the use of raw eggs.
- Use pasteurized eggs if concerned about raw yolks.

Kutia
Polish Christmas Wheat and Poppy Seed Dessert

SERVES: 6 - 8 **PREP TIME: 10 MINS** **COOKING TIME: 1 HOUR** **CHILLING TIME: 30 MINS**

In the Polish tradition, families would toss a spoonful of Kutia onto the ceiling—if it stuck, it was believed to bring good luck and a prosperous harvest in the coming year!

Ingredients

For the Dessert
- **200g (1 cup)** wheat berries (whole wheat kernels)
- **100g (¾ cup)** poppy seeds
- **100g (⅓ cup)** honey
- **50g (⅓ cup)** walnuts, chopped
- **50g (⅓ cup)** almonds, chopped
- **50g (⅓ cup)** raisins or cranberries
- **50g (⅓ cup)** dried figs or apricots
- **1 tsp** vanilla extract (optional)
- **1 tbsp** lemon zest (optional)

For Extra Flavor
- **1–2 tbsp** rum or brandy (optional)
- **Pinch** of cinnamon

Instructions

Cook the Wheat Berries
- Soak wheat berries overnight in cold water to soften.
- Drain, rinse, and transfer to a pot. Cover with fresh water and bring to a boil.
- Simmer for 45–60 minutes until tender but still chewy. Drain and cool.

Prepare the Poppy Seeds
- In a separate pot, boil poppy seeds for 20 minutes, then drain.
- Grind the poppy seeds using a food processor, grinder, or mortar and pestle until creamy.

Mix the Kutia
- In a large bowl, combine cooked wheat, ground poppy seeds, nuts, dried fruits, and lemon zest.
- Stir in honey, vanilla, and rum/brandy (if using).
- Mix well, ensuring the honey coats everything evenly.

Chill and Serve
- Let the kutia sit for at least 1 hour to develop flavors.
- Serve cold in small bowls, garnished with extra nuts or cinnamon.

Storage Tips
- Kutia can be stored in the fridge for up to 3 days.
- The longer it sits, the better the flavors meld together!
- For extra sweetness, drizzle with more honey before serving.

Ryż z Jabłkami
Polish Rice with Apples Dessert

SERVES: 4 **PREP TIME: 10 MINS** **COOKING TIME: 25 MINS** **BAKING TIME: 15 MINS**

This dish was a popular school lunch dessert in Poland, bringing nostalgia to many who remember eating it as children in school cafeterias or at home with their grandparents!

Ingredients

For the Rice
- **200g (1 cup)** white rice (e.g., medium-grain or short-grain)
- **500ml (2 cups)** milk
- **250ml (1 cup)** water
- **2 tbsp** unsalted butter
- **2 tbsp** sugar
- **1 tsp** vanilla extract (optional)
- **Pinch** of salt

For the Apple Layer
- **3-4 medium** apples (Granny Smith, Golden Delicious, or Jonagold)
- **2 tbsp** sugar (adjust based on apple sweetness)
- **1 tsp** cinnamon
- **1 tbsp** lemon juice

Optional Topping
- **1 tbsp** butter (for greasing, if baking)
- **1 tsp** cinnamon sugar
- **Powdered sugar (for serving)**

Instructions

Cook the Rice
- In a saucepan, bring milk, water, butter, sugar, vanilla, and salt to a simmer.
- Add the rice, lower the heat, and cook for 15–20 minutes, stirring occasionally, until soft and creamy.
- Remove from heat and set aside.

Prepare the Apples
- Peel, core, and **grate the apples** (or chop them finely).
- Mix with **sugar, cinnamon, and lemon juice** to prevent browning.

Assemble the Layers
- In individual bowls or a baking dish, layer **half of the cooked rice**.
- Add the **spiced apples** on top.
- Cover with the **remaining rice** and sprinkle with **cinnamon sugar**.

Serve or Bake
- Quick Serve: Eat as-is, warm or chilled.
- Baked Version:
  - Preheat oven to **180°C (350°F)**.
  - Grease a baking dish with butter, layer the rice and apples, and bake for 15 minutes until golden.

Garnish and Enjoy
- Dust with powdered sugar before serving.
- Enjoy warm or cold with a dollop of yogurt or whipped cream if desired!

Storage Tips
- Store in an airtight container in the fridge for up to 3 days.
- Reheat gently on the stove or microwave before serving.
- Try adding raisins or nuts for extra texture.

Ryż z Cynamonem
Polish Rice Pudding with Cinnamon

| SERVES: 4 | PREP TIME: 5 MINS | COOKING TIME: 25 MINS | COOKING TIME: 25 MINS |

In Poland, Ryż z Cynamonem was a popular childhood supper often served by grandparents. It was also a cheap and filling dish during the post-war years, making it a nostalgic comfort food for many Polish families!

Ingredients

For the Rice
- **200g (1 cup)** white rice (short-grain or medium-grain preferred)
- **500ml (2 cups)** milk
- **250ml (1 cup)** water
- **2 tbsp** unsalted butter
- **2 tbsp** sugar (adjust to taste)
- **1 tsp** vanilla extract (optional)
- **1 tsp** ground cinnamon
- **Pinch** of salt

Optional Toppings
- Extra cinnamon sugar for dusting
- Powdered sugar
- Fruit jam (raspberry, strawberry, or plum)
- Whipped cream or yogurt

Instructions

Cook the Rice
- In a saucepan, combine milk, water, butter, sugar, vanilla extract, and salt.
- Bring to a gentle simmer, stirring occasionally.
- Add the rice, lower the heat, and cook for 20-25 minutes, stirring frequently to prevent sticking.

Add Cinnamon
- Once the rice is soft and creamy, stir in **cinnamon**.
- Remove from heat and let rest for **5 minutes** before serving.

Serve
- Spoon the warm rice pudding into bowls.
- Sprinkle with extra **cinnamon sugar or powdered sugar**.
- Add **fruit jam, whipped cream, or yogurt** if desired.

Storage Tips
- Store leftovers in the fridge for up to 3 days.
- Reheat with a splash of milk to restore creaminess.
- For a richer taste, use heavy cream instead of milk.

Ryż na Mleku
Polish Rice Pudding

SERVES: 4 **PREP TIME: 5 MINS** **COOKING TIME: 25 - 30 MINS** **RESTING TIME: 10 MINS**

In Poland, Ryż na Mleku was often served as a childhood supper because it was easy to digest, warm, and filling—making it a favorite meal given by Polish grandmothers to their grandchildren before bedtime!

Ingredients

For the Rice
- **200g (1 cup)** white rice (short-grain or medium-grain)
- **500ml (2 cups)** milk
- **250ml (1 cup)** water
- **2 tbsp** sugar (adjust to taste)
- **2 tbsp** unsalted butter
- **1 tsp** vanilla extract (optional)
- **Pinch** of salt

Optional Toppings
- Cinnamon sugar
- Powdered sugar
- Fruit jam (raspberry, strawberry, or plum)
- Fresh berries
- Cocoa powder or grated chocolate
- Whipped cream or yogurt

Instructions

Cook the Rice
- In a saucepan, combine milk, water, butter, sugar, vanilla extract, and salt.
- Bring to a gentle simmer over medium heat.
- Add the rice, lower the heat, and cook for 20–25 minutes, stirring frequently to prevent sticking.
- Cook until the rice absorbs the liquid and becomes thick and creamy.
- If the pudding becomes too thick, add more **warm milk** to adjust the consistency.
- Once the rice is soft and creamy, stir in **cinnamon**.
- Remove from heat and let rest for **5 minutes** before serving.

Serve
- Spoon the warm rice pudding into bowls.
- Sprinkle with extra cinnamon sugar or cocoa powder.
- Add fruit jam, whipped cream, or yogurt if desired.

Storage Tips
- Store in an airtight container in the fridge for up to 3 days.
- Reheat gently with a splash of milk to restore creaminess.
- For an extra rich flavor, use heavy cream instead of milk.

Kasza Manna na Mleku
Polish Semolina Pudding

SERVES: 2 **PREP TIME: 5 MINS** **COOKING TIME: 5 MINS** **COOKING TIME: 5 MINS**

In Poland, Kasza Manna was a popular childhood dish, often given to kids as a comforting meal before bedtime. Many Poles have nostalgic memories of their grandmothers making this warm and creamy dessert!

Ingredients

For the Pudding
- **500ml (2 cups)** milk
- **50g (¼ cup)** semolina (kasza manna)
- **2 tbsp sugar (adjust to taste)**
- **1 tsp** vanilla extract (optional)
- **1 tbsp** butter (optional, for extra creaminess)
- **Pinch** of salt

Optional Toppings
- Cinnamon sugar
- Cocoa powder or grated chocolate
- Fruit jam (strawberry, raspberry, plum)
- Fresh berries
- Honey or maple syrup

Instructions

Heat the Milk
- In a saucepan, heat the milk over medium heat until it begins to simmer.
- Stir in sugar, vanilla extract, and a pinch of salt.

Cook the Semolina
- Slowly pour the semolina (kasza manna) into the milk while stirring continuously to prevent lumps.
- Cook on low heat for about 3–5 minutes, stirring constantly until the mixture thickens.
- If using, stir in butter at the end for a smoother texture.

Serve
- Pour the warm semolina pudding into bowls.
- Sprinkle with cinnamon sugar, cocoa powder, or drizzle with fruit jam.
- Enjoy warm.

Storage Tips
- Best enjoyed fresh, but can be stored in the fridge for 1–2 days.
- Reheat with a splash of milk to restore creaminess.
- For a more indulgent version, replace part of the milk with cream.

Zupa Owocowa
Polish Fruit Soup

| SERVES: 4 | PREP TIME: 10 MINS | COOKING TIME: 15 MINS | CHILLING TIME: 15 MINS |

In Polish tradition, Zupa Owocowa was often served in schools and summer camps as a light lunch during hot days. It was considered a special treat, especially when made with fresh-picked berries from the garden!

Ingredients

For the Soup
- **500g (2–3 cups)** fresh or frozen fruit (strawberries, cherries, raspberries, blueberries, apples, or plums)
- **1L (4 cups)** water
- **3 tbsp** sugar (adjust to taste**)**
- **1 tbsp** lemon juice (optional)
- **1** cinnamon stick **or ½ tsp** ground
- **2** cloves (optional**)**
- **1 tbsp** potato starch or cornstarch (for thickening, optional)

Optional Toppings
- Cooked pasta (thin noodles, macaroni, or egg noodles)
- Cooked rice
- Croutons or whipped cream for extra richness

Instructions

Cook the Fruit
- In a saucepan, combine water, sugar, cinnamon, cloves (if using), and fruit.
- Bring to a boil, then simmer for 10 minutes until the fruit softens.

Blend and Thicken (Optional)
- Remove cinnamon and cloves.
- If you prefer a smooth soup, blend the fruit mixture with a hand blender.
- To thicken, mix 1 tbsp cornstarch with 2 tbsp cold water, then stir it into the soup and cook for 2 minutes until slightly thickened.

Serve
- Serve warm or chilled in bowls.
- Add cooked pasta, rice, or croutons for extra texture.
- For a sweeter touch, top with whipped cream or a drizzle of honey.

Storage Tips
- Store in the fridge for up to 3 days.
- Enjoy cold during summer or warm in winter with extra spices like nutmeg.

Lody Śmietankowe
Polish-Style Vanilla Ice Cream

SERVES: 6 SCOOPS   **PREP TIME: 10 MINS**   **CHILLING TIME: 3 - 4 HOURS**

In Poland, Lody Śmietankowe was one of the first ice cream flavors sold in pre-war Polish cafés and was considered a luxury treat! Before refrigeration, ice was harvested from lakes and stored in underground ice houses to make ice cream year-round.

Ingredients

For the Ice Cream
- **500ml (2 cups)** heavy cream (30–36% fat)
- **250ml (1 cup)** whole milk
- **4 large** egg yolks
- **100g (½ cup)** granulated sugar
- **1 tsp** vanilla extract or seeds from 1 vanilla bean

Optional Toppings
- Crushed nuts (almonds, hazelnuts)
- Chocolate chips
- • Fruit purée (strawberry, raspberry, or blueberry)

Instructions

Heat the Milk and Cream
- In a saucepan, heat cream, milk, and vanilla extract over medium heat until it begins to steam (but not boil).

Prepare the Egg Mixture
- In a separate bowl, whisk egg yolks and sugar until pale and creamy.
- Slowly pour half of the warm milk mixture into the egg yolks, whisking continuously to prevent curdling.

Cook the Custard
- Pour the egg mixture back into the saucepan with the remaining milk.
- Cook over low heat, stirring constantly until the mixture thickens (about 5 minutes). Do not let it boil!
- Once it coats the back of a spoon, remove from heat and let it cool to room temperature.

Chill and Freeze
- Pour the mixture into a container and refrigerate for at least 3 hours until completely chilled.
- If using an ice cream maker, churn according to instructions.
- If making without an ice cream maker, place in the freezer and stir every 30 minutes for 3 hours to prevent ice crystals.

Serve
- Scoop into bowls or cones.
- Garnish with **chocolate shavings, fruit, or caramel sauce**.

Storage Tips
- Store in an airtight container in the freezer for up to 1 week.
- For a softer texture, let sit at room temperature for 5 minutes before scooping.

Lody Truskawkowe
Polish-Style Strawberry Ice Cream

SERVES: 6 SCOOPS   **PREP TIME: 15 MINS**   **CHILLING TIME: 3 - 4 HOURS**

Poland is one of Europe's top strawberry producers, and Polish strawberries are famous for their intense sweetness! Many families in Poland traditionally make strawberry ice cream at home every summer using fresh-picked berries from local farms or gardens.

Ingredients

For the Ice Cream
- **300g (2 cups)** fresh strawberries, hulled
- **100g (½ cup)** granulated sugar
- **1 tbsp** lemon juice (optional, enhances flavor)
- **250ml (1 cup)** heavy cream (30–36% fat)
- **250ml (1 cup)** whole milk
- **3 large** egg yolks
- **1 tsp** vanilla extract

Optional Toppings
- Chopped strawberries for extra texture
- White or dark chocolate chips
- Strawberry jam swirl

Instructions

Prepare the Strawberry Purée
- Blend strawberries, sugar, and lemon juice in a food processor until smooth.
- Strain through a sieve if you prefer a smoother texture.

Heat the Milk and Cream
- In a saucepan, heat milk, heavy cream, and vanilla extract over medium heat until steaming (but do not boil).

Prepare the Egg Mixture
- In a separate bowl, whisk egg yolks and 2 tbsp sugar until pale and creamy.
- Slowly pour half of the warm milk mixture into the egg yolks, whisking continuously to prevent curdling.

Cook the Custard
- Pour the egg mixture back into the saucepan.
- Cook over low heat, stirring constantly until the mixture thickens (about 5 minutes). Do not let it boil!
- Remove from heat and let cool.

Combine and Chill
- Stir the strawberry purée into the cooled custard mixture.
- Refrigerate for at least 3 hours until completely chilled.

Freeze the Ice Cream
- **With an Ice Cream Maker:** Churn according to manufacturer instructions.
- **Without an Ice Cream Maker:**
  - Pour the mixture into a container and freeze.
  - Stir every **30 minutes for 3 hours** to prevent ice crystals.

Serve
- Scoop into bowls or cones.
- Garnish with **fresh strawberries, chocolate shavings, or whipped cream.**

Storage Tips
- Store in an airtight container in the freezer for up to 1 week.
- Let sit at room temperature for 5 minutes before scooping for a softer texture.

Lody Waniliowe
Polish-Style Vanilla Ice Cream

SERVES: 6 SCOOPS **PREP TIME: 10 MINS** **CHILLING TIME: 3 - 4 HOURS**

In Poland, Lody Waniliowe was traditionally made in wooden ice cream churns, using natural vanilla imported from Madagascar. In the past, ice was harvested from lakes and stored in ice houses to keep the ice cream cold all year long!

Ingredients

For the Ice Cream
- 500ml (2 cups) heavy cream (30–36% fat)
- 250ml (1 cup) whole milk
- 4 large egg yolks
- 100g (½ cup) granulated sugar
- 1 vanilla bean **(or 1½ tsp** vanilla extract**)**

Optional Toppings
- Crushed nuts (almonds, walnuts)
- Chocolate chips
- Fresh berries or fruit puree

Instructions

Heat the Milk and Cream
- In a saucepan, combine heavy cream and milk.
- Slice vanilla bean lengthwise, scrape out seeds, and add both seeds and pod to the milk mixture.
- Heat over medium heat until steaming, but do not let it boil. Remove from heat and let infuse for 10 minutes.

Prepare the Egg Mixture
- In a separate bowl, whisk egg yolks and sugar until pale and creamy.
- Slowly pour half of the warm milk mixture into the egg yolks, whisking continuously to prevent curdling.

Cook the Custard
- Pour the egg mixture back into the saucepan.
- Cook over low heat, stirring constantly until the mixture thickens (about 5 minutes). Do not let it boil!
- Remove from heat and let cool.

Freeze the Ice Cream
- **With an Ice Cream Maker:** Churn according to manufacturer instructions.
- **Without an Ice Cream Maker:**
  - Pour the mixture into a container and freeze.
  - Stir every **30 minutes for 3 hours** to prevent ice crystals.

Serve
- Scoop into bowls or cones.
- Garnish with **fresh strawberries, chocolate sauce, or caramel drizzle**

Storage Tips
- Store in an airtight container in the freezer for up to 1 week.
- Let sit at room temperature for 5 minutes before scooping for a softer texture.

Kompot z Suszu
Polish Dried Fruit Compote

SERVES: 6 - 8 **PREP TIME: 5 MINS** **COOKING TIME: 30 MINS** **CHILLING TIME: 30 MINS**

In Poland, Kompot z Suszu is believed to aid digestion, which is helpful after a big Christmas Eve feast! Some say it also brings good luck and prosperity for the new year.

Ingredients

For the Compote
- **200g (1½ cups)** dried apples
- **200g (1½ cups)** dried pears
- **100g (¾ cup)** dried prunes
- **100g (¾ cup)** dried apricots
- **1.5L (6 cups)** water
- **3 tbsp** honey or sugar (adjust to taste)
- **1** cinnamon stick
- **3** cloves
- **1** star anise (optional)
- **1 tsp** lemon zest (optional)
- **Juice of 1** lemon (optional, for tartness)

Optional Add-Ins
- Raisins or dried figs
- A splash of apple juice for extra sweetness
- A pinch of nutmeg

Instructions

Prepare the Ingredients
- Rinse the dried fruits under cold water to remove any dust.
- If the dried fruits are very hard, soak them in warm water for 15 minutes to soften.

Cook the Compote
- In a large pot, bring water, dried fruits, cinnamon stick, cloves, and star anise to a gentle boil.
- Reduce heat and simmer for 30 minutes, stirring occasionally.
- Add honey (or sugar), lemon zest, and lemon juice. Stir well.
- Remove from heat and let it sit for at least 30 minutes to enhance the flavors.

Serve
- Strain the compote for a clear drink, or serve it with the rehydrated fruits.
- Enjoy warm or chilled, depending on preference.
- Serve with a slice of orange for extra festive flavor.

Storage Tips
- Store in the fridge for up to 5 days. The flavors develop better overnight.

Gofry
Traditional Polish Waffles

SERVES: 6 WAFFLES **PREP TIME: 10 MINS** **COOKING TIME: 10 MINS**

In Poland, Gofry are a popular seaside snack, especially in resorts along the Baltic Sea, where they are often sold at beachside stalls with piles of whipped cream and fresh fruit!

Ingredients

For the Waffles
- **250g (2 cups)** all-purpose flour
- **2 tbsp** sugar
- **2 tsp** baking powder
- **1/2 tsp** salt
- **2 large** eggs (separated)
- **300ml (1¼ cups)** milk
- **100g (7 tbsp)** unsalted butter, melted
- **1 tsp** vanilla extract

Optional Toppings
- Powdered sugar
- Whipped cream
- Fresh berries (strawberries, blueberries, raspberries)
- Chocolate sauce or Nutella
- Ice cream

Instructions

Prepare the Batter
- In a large bowl, mix flour, sugar, baking powder, and salt.
- In a separate bowl, whisk together egg yolks, milk, melted butter, and vanilla extract.
- Gradually mix the wet ingredients into the dry ingredients until smooth.

Whip the Egg Whites
- In another bowl, beat **egg whites** until stiff peaks form.
- Gently fold the whipped egg whites into the batter to keep it light and airy.

Cook the Waffles
- Preheat a **waffle iron** and grease it lightly with butter or oil.
- Pour **about ½ cup** of batter into the waffle iron.
- Close the lid and cook for **3–5 minutes** until golden and crisp.
- Repeat with the remaining batter.
- Serve with powdered sugar or toppings.
- Add **cinnamon or lemon zest** for extra flavor!

Storage Tips
- Store leftovers in the fridge for up to 2 days or freeze for up to 1 month.
- Reheat in a toaster or oven for extra crispiness

Ciepłe Lody
Polish "Warm Ice Cream"

SERVES: 6 - 8 **PREP TIME: 15 MINS** **COOKING TIME: 5 MINS** **CHILLING TIME: 30 MINS**

During the Polish communist era, real ice cream was hard to find in winter, so Ciepłe Lody became a popular substitute, sold in bakeries and kiosks as a special sweet treat!

Ingredients

For the Meringue Filling
- **3 large** egg whites
- **150g (¾ cup)** granulated sugar
- **75ml (⅓ cup)** water
- **½ tsp** lemon juice
- **1 tsp** vanilla extract

For the Chocolate Glaze
- **100g (3.5 oz)** dark chocolate
- **2 tbsp** butter or heavy cream

For Serving
- **6–8** wafer cups or small glasses
- Sprinkles, chopped nuts, or coconut flakes (optional)

Instructions

Prepare the Meringue Filling
- In a small saucepan, heat sugar and water over medium heat, stirring until fully dissolved.
- Bring to a gentle boil and cook until it reaches 115–120°C (240–250°F) (soft ball stage).
- In a separate bowl, beat egg whites with lemon juice until soft peaks form.
- Slowly pour the hot sugar syrup into the egg whites while beating on high speed.
- Continue whipping for 5 minutes, until the mixture is thick, glossy, and holds firm peaks.
- Mix in vanilla extract.

Fill the Wafer Cups
- Using a piping bag (or spoon), fill wafer cups or small glasses with the meringue mixture.
- Smooth the tops and chill in the refrigerator for 30 minutes.

Prepare the Chocolate Glaze
- Melt chocolate and butter/cream over low heat, stirring until smooth.
- Let it cool slightly before pouring over the meringue.

Decorate and Serve
- Drizzle or dip the **tops of the filled cups** in the chocolate glaze.
- Sprinkle with **chopped nuts, coconut, or sprinkles** if desired.
- Let set for **5–10 minutes**, then serve immediately or refrigerate until ready to eat.
- Try different flavors by adding cocoa powder, fruit puree, or coffee extract to the meringue!

Storage Tips
- Best enjoyed fresh, but can be stored in the fridge for 1–2 days.
- Use a kitchen thermometer for the sugar syrup to ensure the perfect consistency.

Krówki
Traditional Polish Fudge

SERVES: 30 PIECES   **PREP TIME: 10 MINS**   **COOKING TIME: 40 MINS**   **COOLING TIME: 2 HOURS**

The first Krówki were made in the early 20th century in Poznań by Feliks Pomorski, whose family recipe became Poland's most famous fudge! Traditional Krówki wrappers still feature a small cow illustration, honoring their original branding.

Ingredients

For the Fudge
- **500ml (2 cups)** full-fat milk
- **200g (1 cup)** sugar
- **100g (7 tbsp)** unsalted butter
- **1 tbsp** honey (optional, for extra creaminess)
- **1 tsp** vanilla extract (optional)

Instructions

Cook the Caramel Mixture
- In a heavy-bottomed saucepan, heat milk, sugar, butter, and honey over medium heat.
- Stir constantly until the sugar dissolves and the butter melts.
- Bring to a gentle boil, then reduce heat to low.

Thicken the Fudge
- Continue **simmering and stirring** for **30–40 minutes**, until the mixture thickens and turns golden brown.
- Add **vanilla extract**, if using, and stir well.
- To check consistency, drop a small amount onto a **cold plate**—it should thicken into a **soft caramel texture**.

Set and Cut the Fudge
- Pour the hot mixture into a greased or parchment-lined baking dish.
- Let cool at room temperature for about 2 hours until firm.
- Cut into small rectangles or squares.

Serve

Storage and Tips
- If you prefer soft Krówki, cook for a shorter time (~30 min).
- For harder, chewy Krówki, cook slightly longer (~45 min).
- Stir constantly to prevent burning.

Chałwa
Polish-Style Halva

SERVES: 10 SLICES **PREP TIME: 15 MINS** **COOLING TIME: 2 - 3 HOURS**

In Poland, chałwa has been produced commercially since the early 20th century, with Warszawska Chałwa becoming one of the most famous brands. It's especially popular in holiday gift boxes and is often enjoyed alongside strong Polish coffee!

Ingredients

For the Halva
- **200g (¾ cup)** tahini (sesame paste)
- **100g (½ cup)** sugar
- **80ml (⅓ cup)** honey
- **½ tsp** vanilla extract (optional)
- **Pinch** of salt
- **50g (⅓ cup)** chopped nuts (walnuts, almonds, or pistachios)

Optional Add-Ins
- **2 tbsp** cocoa powder for chocolate halva
- **½ tsp** cinnamon for a spiced version

Instructions

Heat the Syrup
- In a small saucepan, heat sugar and honey over low-medium heat.
- Stir constantly until the sugar dissolves and the mixture reaches 115–120°C (240–250°F) (soft-ball stage).
- Remove from heat and let cool for 1–2 minutes.

Mix with Tahini
- In a separate bowl, whisk together tahini, vanilla extract, and salt.
- Slowly pour the warm syrup into the tahini, stirring quickly but gently until fully combined.
- Mix in chopped nuts (or cocoa/cinnamon if using).

Shape and Cool
- Pour the mixture into a small parchment-lined loaf pan or mold.
- Press it down evenly, smoothing the top.
- Let it cool at room temperature for 2–3 hours until firm.
- Slice and sprinkle with nuts.

Storage Tips
- Store in an airtight container at room temperature for up to 2 weeks.
- For firmer chałwa, let it rest overnight before cutting.

Cukierki Mleczne
Polish Milk Candies

SERVES: 30 PIECES **PREP TIME: 5 MINS** **COOKING TIME: 30 MINS** **COOLING TIME: 1 - 2 HOURS**

Polish milk candies were a popular homemade treat during communist Poland, as store-bought sweets were often limited. Many families made their own versions using just milk, sugar, and butter to satisfy their sweet cravings!

Ingredients

For the Candy
- **500ml (2 cups)** full-fat milk
- **200g (1 cup)** granulated sugar
- **100g (7 tbsp)** unsalted butter
- **2 tbsp** honey (optional, for extra smoothness)
- **1 tsp** vanilla extract (optional)

Instructions

Cook the Milk Mixture
- In a heavy-bottomed saucepan, combine milk, sugar, butter, and honey.
- Heat over medium-low heat, stirring constantly until the sugar dissolves and butter melts.

Simmer Until Thickened
- Bring the mixture to a gentle simmer, stirring frequently.
- Cook for 25–30 minutes, stirring often, until the mixture turns golden brown and thickens.
- Add vanilla extract and mix well.

Pour and Cool
- Pour the hot candy mixture into a parchment-lined baking dish.
- Let cool at room temperature for 1–2 hours until firm.

Cut and Serve
- Once set, cut into small squares or rectangles.
- Wrap in wax paper for a traditional touch.

Storage Tips
- Store in an airtight container at room temperature for up to 2 weeks.
- For harder candies, cook longer (~35 minutes).
- For softer caramels, reduce cooking time slightly.

Śliwki w Czekoladzie
Polish Chocolate-Covered Plums

SERVES: 20 PIECES **PREP TIME: 10 MINS** **COOKING TIME: 30 MINS**

These chocolate-covered plums have been a Polish delicacy since the 19th century, often given as luxury gifts. Today, they are still a popular Polish souvenir, especially from cities like Kraków and Warsaw!

Ingredients

For the Plums
- **200g (1 cup)** dried plums (prunes), preferably soft and juicy
- **150g (5 oz)** dark chocolate (at least 60% cocoa)
- **1 tbsp** butter or heavy cream (for extra smoothness)

Optional Add-Ins
- Marzipan (for stuffing the plums)
- Rum or brandy (soak plums for 1 hour for an extra kick)
- Chopped nuts (walnuts or almonds for garnish)

Instructions

Prepare the Plums
- If using rum or brandy, soak the dried plums for 1 hour, then drain and pat dry.
- If filling with marzipan, stuff each plum with a small piece of marzipan.

Melt the Chocolate
- Break the dark chocolate into pieces.
- In a heatproof bowl, melt the chocolate with butter or cream over a double boiler (or microwave in short bursts).
- Stir until smooth and glossy.

Dip the Plums
- Using a **fork or skewer**, dip each dried plum into the melted chocolate.
- Let **excess chocolate drip off**, then place on a parchment-lined tray.
- If using **chopped nuts**, sprinkle them over the plums before the chocolate sets.

Chill and Serve
- Refrigerate for **30 minutes.**

Storage Tips
- Store in an airtight container in the fridge for up to 2 weeks.
- For a smoother chocolate texture, temper the chocolate before dipping.
- Try using white chocolate or milk chocolate for variation!

Pierniki Toruńskie
Traditional Polish Toruń Gingerbread

SERVES: 20 COOKIES **PREP TIME:** 20 MINS + 2 HOURS CHILLING TIME **BAKING TIME:** 10 - 12 MINS

Toruń's gingerbread has been famous since the 13th century, and it was so prized that Polish kings and queens used it as a diplomatic gift! Today, you can visit the Toruń Gingerbread Museum, where you can bake your own Pierniki Toruńskie!

Ingredients

For the Gingerbread Dough
- **500g (4 cups)** all-purpose flour
- **200g (1 cup)** honey
- **150g (¾ cup)** brown sugar
- **120g (½ cup)** unsalted butter
- **1 large** egg
- **1 tsp** baking soda
- **2 tbsp** cocoa powder (optional
- **2 tsp** gingerbread spice mix
- **1 tsp** cinnamon
- **Pinch** of salt

Gingerbread Spice Mix
- **1 tsp** ground ginger
- **1 tsp** ground cloves
- **½ tsp** ground nutmeg
- **½ tsp** ground allspice
- **½ tsp** ground cardamom

Chocolate Glaze (Optional)
- **100g (3.5 oz)** dark chocolate
- **2 tbsp** butter

Icing (Optional)
- **100g (¾ cup)** powdered sugar
- **2 tbsp** milk or lemon juice

Instructions

Prepare the Dough
- In a saucepan, melt honey, brown sugar, and butter over low heat until smooth. Let cool slightly.
- In a bowl, mix flour, baking soda, cocoa (if using), spices, cinnamon, and salt.
- Add the warm honey mixture and the egg to the dry ingredients. Mix well.
- Knead into a smooth dough (if sticky, chill for 30 minutes before kneading).
- Wrap in plastic and refrigerate for at least 2 hours (or overnight for deeper flavor).

Roll and Cut the Cookies
- Preheat oven to 180°C (350°F).
- Roll out the dough on a floured surface to 5mm (¼ inch) thickness.
- Cut into hearts, stars, or traditional shapes.
- Place on a parchment-lined baking sheet.

Bake the Gingerbread
- Bake for 10–12 minutes, until slightly firm but still soft.
- 2. Let cool completely before decorating.

Decorate the Pierniki
- **Chocolate Glaze:**
  - Melt **chocolate and butter** over low heat.
  - Dip the cookies or drizzle with chocolate. Let set.
- **Sugar Icing:**
  - Mix **powdered sugar with milk or lemon juice** until smooth.
  - Pipe designs onto the cookies using a **piping bag or spoon**.

Storage Tips
- Store in an airtight container for up to 3 weeks (they soften over time!).
- For softer gingerbread, add a slice of apple to the container.
- Try filling with plum jam for an authentic Toruń-style variation.

Blok Czekoladowy
Polish No-Bake Chocolate Block

SERVES: 12 - 15 SLICES **PREP TIME: 15 MINS** **CHILLING TIME: 2 - 3 HOURS**

During communist Poland, real chocolate was often unavailable, so Blok Czekoladowy became a homemade substitute that satisfied sweet cravings without real chocolate! It remains a nostalgic treat for many Poles today.

Ingredients

For the Block
- 200g (7 oz) unsalted butter
- 200g (1 cup) sugar
- 120ml (½ cup) water or milk
- 50g (½ cup) unsweetened cocoa powder
- 400g (3½ cups) powdered milk
- 200g (7 oz) crushed tea biscuits (Petit Beurre or Digestive)
- 50g (⅓ cup) chopped nuts
- 1 tsp vanilla extract (optional)

Optional Add-Ins
- Raisins or dried fruit
- Shredded coconut
- Marshmallows

Instructions

Prepare the Chocolate Mixture
- In a saucepan over low heat, melt butter, sugar, and water (or milk) until fully dissolved.
- Stir in cocoa powder and vanilla extract, mixing until smooth. Remove from heat.

Add the Dry Ingredients
- In a large bowl, combine powdered milk, crushed biscuits, and nuts.
- Pour the warm chocolate mixture over the dry ingredients and stir quickly until fully combined.

Shape the Block
- Transfer the mixture to a parchment-lined loaf pan or rectangular mold.
- Press down firmly to even out the surface.

Chill and Serve
- Refrigerate for 2–3 hours until firm.
- Once set, slice into small squares or bars and serve.

Storage Tips
- Store in the fridge for up to 1 week.
- For a firmer texture, chill overnight.
- Try using white chocolate powder instead of cocoa for a vanilla version!

Sezamki
Polish Sesame Seed Brittle

| SERVES: 20 PIECES | PREP TIME: 5 MINS | COOKING TIME: 10 MINS | COOLING TIME: 30 MINS |

Sezamki became popular in Poland due to Jewish and Middle Eastern influences, and they were often sold at markets or kiosks as a healthier alternative to regular candy!

Ingredients

For the Brittle

- **200g (1 cup)** sesame seeds
- **150g (¾ cup)** sugar
- **2 tbsp** honey
- **1 tbsp** unsalted butter (optional, for extra richness)
- **Pinch** of salt
- **½ tsp** vanilla extract (optional)

Instructions

Toast the Sesame Seeds

- In a dry pan over medium heat, toast the sesame seeds for 3–4 minutes, stirring constantly until golden and fragrant.
- Remove from heat and set aside.

Make the Caramel

- In a saucepan over medium-low heat, melt sugar and honey together, stirring occasionally.
- Cook until the sugar dissolves and turns into a golden caramel (about 5 minutes).
- Add butter, salt, and vanilla extract (if using), stirring until smooth.

Combine and Shape

- Quickly stir in the toasted sesame seeds, mixing well to coat them in the caramel.
- Pour the mixture onto a parchment-lined baking sheet.
- Using a rolling pin or spatula, flatten the mixture into a thin, even layer.

Cool and Cut

- Let cool for 30 minutes until firm.
- Once set, cut into bars or break into bite-sized pieces.
- Try adding chopped nuts (almonds, peanuts) or a drizzle of dark chocolate.

Storage Tips

- Store in an airtight container at room temperature for up to 2 weeks.
- To prevent sticking, layer with parchment paper.

Krem Krówkowy
Polish Caramel Cream Spread

| SERVES: 1 CUP | PREP TIME: 5 MINS | COOKING TIME: 15 MINS | COOLING TIME: 30 MINS |

This caramel spread is inspired by Krówki, Poland's famous soft fudge candies! The first Krówki were made in the early 20th century, and their signature creamy, gooey center inspired this delicious caramel spread.

Ingredients

For the Spread
- **1 can (400g)** sweetened condensed milk
- **100g (½ cup)** brown sugar
- **50g (3½ tbsp)** unsalted butter
- **1 tsp** vanilla extract
- **Pinch** of salt

Instructions

Melt the Sugar and Butter
- In a saucepan, melt butter and brown sugar over low heat, stirring constantly.
- Cook until the sugar dissolves and turns golden brown (about 3 minutes).

Cook the Caramel Cream
- Slowly pour in the sweetened condensed milk, stirring continuously.
- Increase heat to medium-low and cook for 10–12 minutes, stirring constantly to prevent burning.
- Add vanilla extract and a pinch of salt.

Cool and Store
- Once the mixture thickens to a spreadable consistency, remove from heat.
- Let cool for 30 minutes, then transfer to a jar.
- Store in the fridge for up to 2 weeks.

Serve on toast, pancakes, or waffles. Or use as a cake filling or dip for fruit.

Storage and Tips
- If too thick after cooling, warm slightly before using.
- For a richer caramel flavor, cook for an extra 5 minutes.
- Try adding a pinch of sea salt for a salted caramel version.

Zefiry
Polish Marshmallow-Like Sweets

| SERVES: 20 PIECES | PREP TIME: 20 MINS | COOKING TIME: 10 MINS | SETTING TIME: 4 - 6 HOURS |

Zefiry were inspired by French meringues but adapted with agar-agar instead of gelatin, giving them their unique soft and airy texture. In Poland, they are often enjoyed with tea or coffee as a light, sweet treat!

Ingredients

For the Zefiry Base
- **200g (1 cup)** fruit purée (apples, strawberries, or raspberries)
- **150g (¾ cup)** granulated sugar
- **1 tbsp** lemon juice
- **2 large** egg whites
- **1 tsp** vanilla extract (optional)

For the Syrup
- **150g (¾ cup)** granulated sugar
- **60ml (¼ cup)** water
- **5g (1½ tsp)** agar-agar (or 10g gelatin dissolved in ¼ cup hot water)

For Dusting
- Powdered sugar

Instructions

Prepare the Fruit Purée
- Blend apples, strawberries, or raspberries into a smooth purée.
- In a saucepan, heat the purée with sugar and lemon juice, stirring until thickened.
- Let cool completely.

Whip the Egg Whites
- In a clean bowl, beat **egg whites** until soft peaks form.
- Add the **cooled fruit purée** and continue beating until fluffy.

Make the Syrup
- In a saucepan, heat **sugar, water, and agar-agar (or gelatin)** over medium heat.
- Stir continuously and cook until the mixture reaches **110°C (230°F)** (soft-ball stage).

Combine and Pipe the Zefiry
- Slowly pour the hot syrup into the egg white mixture while beating continuously.
- Continue beating for 5 minutes, until the mixture thickens and holds its shape.
- Transfer to a piping bag and pipe swirls onto parchment paper.

Set and Serve
- Let sit at **room temperature for 4–6 hours** until firm.
- Dust with **powdered sugar** before serving.

Storage and Tips
- Store in an airtight container at room temperature for up to 5 days.
- For a chocolate version, dip in melted dark chocolate.
- Use different fruit purées for color variations!

Lukrowane Orzeszki
Polish Sugared Nuts

SERVES: 4 CUPS　　**PREP TIME: 5 MINS**　　**COOKING TIME: 10 - 15 MINS**

Sugared nuts were a favorite treat of Polish nobility in the 17th century, often served during royal feasts and special celebrations! Today, they are a staple at Christmas markets and fairs across Poland.

Ingredients

For the Nuts
- **200g (2 cups)** nuts (almonds, walnuts, or hazelnuts)
- **100g (½ cup)** granulated sugar
- **2 tbsp** honey (optional, for extra flavor)
- **1 tsp** cinnamon (optional)
- **1 tsp** vanilla extract
- **Pinch** of salt
- **2 tbsp** water

Instructions

Heat the Sugar Mixture
- In a non-stick pan over medium heat, combine sugar, honey, cinnamon, vanilla extract, salt, and water.
- Stir continuously until the sugar melts and forms a thick syrup.

Coat the Nuts
- Add the **nuts** to the pan and stir quickly to coat them evenly.
- Continue cooking for **5–7 minutes**, stirring constantly, until the sugar caramelizes and hardens around the nuts.

Cool and Serve
- Transfer the nuts to a **parchment-lined tray** and separate them with a fork.
- Let cool completely before serving.

Storage and Tips
- Store in an airtight container at room temperature for up to 2 weeks.
- For extra crunch, bake at 150°C (300°F) for 5 minutes after coating.
- Try using different nuts or adding nutmeg for extra spice!

Cukierki Truflowe
Polish Truffle Candies

SERVES: 20 TRUFFLES **PREP TIME: 15 MINS** **CHILLING TIME: 1 - 2 HOURS**

These truffles were a popular homemade alternative to expensive chocolates in Poland during the communist era, when luxury sweets were hard to find. Homemakers created their own versions using basic pantry ingredients!

Ingredients

For the Candies
- **200g (7 oz)** dark chocolate (70% cocoa or more)
- **100g (7 tbsp)** unsalted butter
- **200g (¾ cup)** sweetened condensed milk
- **2 tbsp** cocoa powder
- **100g (1 cup)** crushed tea biscuits (e.g., Petit Beurre)
- **1 tsp** vanilla extract
- **Pinch** of salt

For the Coating (Optional)
- Cocoa powder
- Shredded coconut
- Chopped nuts (hazelnuts, almonds, or walnuts)

Instructions

Melt the Chocolate Mixture
- In a heatproof bowl, melt the dark chocolate and butter over a double boiler (or microwave in 30-second intervals).
- Stir in sweetened condensed milk, cocoa powder, vanilla extract, and salt until smooth.

Add the Biscuits
- Crush tea biscuits into fine crumbs and mix them into the chocolate mixture.
- Stir well until combined and let cool slightly.

Shape the Truffles
- Using a teaspoon or small scoop, roll the mixture into small balls (~2cm in diameter).
- Roll each truffle in cocoa powder, coconut, or chopped nuts.

Chill and Serve
- Place the truffles on a **parchment-lined tray** and refrigerate for **1–2 hours** until firm.

Storage Tips
- Store in the fridge for up to 1 week.
- For a boozy version, add 1 tbsp rum or coffee liqueur.
- Try mixing in orange zest or instant coffee for extra flavor!

Ptasie Mleczko
Polish Marshmallow-Like Chocolate-Covered Treat

SERVES: 20 PIECES   **PREP TIME: 30 MINS**   **CHILLING TIME: 3 - 4 HOURS**

The name "Ptasie Mleczko" means "Bird's Milk", which in Polish folklore symbolizes something incredibly rare and luxurious. Today, it remains one of Poland's most famous chocolate treats, exported worldwide!

Ingredients

For the Marshmallow Base
- **300ml (1¼ cups)** milk
- **200ml (¾ cup)** heavy cream (30% fat or more)
- **150g (¾ cup)** sugar
- **2 tsp** vanilla extract
- **10g (3½ tsp)** gelatin powder
- **60ml (¼ cup)** cold water

For the Chocolate Coating
- **200g (7 oz)** dark chocolate (at least 60% cocoa)
- **2 tbsp** butter or coconut oil (for shine and smoothness)

Instructions

Prepare the Gelatin
- In a small bowl, sprinkle gelatin over cold water and let it sit for 5–10 minutes to bloom.

Heat the Milk Mixture
- In a saucepan, heat milk, heavy cream, sugar, and vanilla extract over medium heat.
- Stir until sugar is fully dissolved but do not boil.

Combine with Gelatin
- Remove the saucepan from heat and stir in the bloomed gelatin.
- Mix until completely dissolved, then let cool to room temperature.

Whip for Fluffiness
- Using a hand mixer, whip the cooled mixture for 5–10 minutes, until it becomes light and airy.
- Pour into a parchment-lined rectangular baking dish and smooth the surface.
- Chill in the fridge for 3–4 hours, until firm.

Prepare the Chocolate Coating
- Melt dark chocolate and butter/coconut oil in a heatproof bowl over a double boiler or microwave.
- Stir until smooth and glossy.

Cut and Coat the Ptasie Mleczko
- Remove the set marshmallow from the fridge and cut into squares or rectangles.
- Dip each piece in melted chocolate using a fork or skewer, ensuring full coverage.
- Place on a parchment-lined tray and refrigerate for 30 minutes to set.

Storage Tips
- Use white or milk chocolate for different flavors.
- Add strawberry or raspberry purée for a fruity twist.
- Coat in cocoa powder or shredded coconut instead of chocolate for variation!

Chapter Five

Conclusion

As you reach the end of this book—crumbs on your counter, sweet smells lingering in the kitchen, and perhaps a plate of warm cookies cooling by the window—I hope you're feeling not just satisfied but connected.

Connected to the flavors of a heritage that's steeped in tradition and love. Connected to the hands that once kneaded dough in a quiet village kitchen. Connected to **Dziadzia Gienek**, who never sought fame or praise but whose desserts made people feel seen, welcome, and cared for.

More than anything, I hope you feel connected to *yourself*—to that quiet part inside that finds peace in mixing batter, joy in watching something rise, and purpose in creating something with your own two hands.

While these 91 recipes are deeply rooted in my grandfather's legacy, they belong to you now too.

Baking as a Bridge

Food is a bridge between generations. It carries voices from the past into our present lives, and every time we recreate a dish, we honor that journey. Whether you grew up hearing the word "dziadzia" or this is your first taste of Polish desserts, you've stepped into a story that's bigger than any one person or kitchen.

You've become part of a long line of bakers who believe in the power of *simple ingredients* turned into something special. In a world that often rushes toward what's new and next, you've chosen to slow down and reach back.

There's something sacred about that.

These recipes, as comforting as they are, do more than feed the body. They feed memory. They feed legacy. They feed a kind of joy that doesn't shout—but hums quietly, like a lullaby passed down from your grandparents.

So whether you're baking **makowiec** for the first time or serving **pączki** on Fat Thursday, know that you're doing more than making dessert—you're keeping a tradition alive.

A Book of Memories, A Book of Invitations

When I first started writing this book, my goal was simple: To gather Dziadzia Gienek's recipes in one place so they wouldn't be lost to time. But somewhere along the way, this became much more than a collection of ingredients and instructions.

It became a *conversation*. Between the past and the present. Between the cook and the table. Between you and someone you may one day pass this book to.

This is not a cookbook to be left on a shelf. It's meant to be used. Dog-eared. Dusted with flour. Stained with jam. It's a book meant to sit open on the counter while little hands help shape cookies, or while old friends sip tea and ask for "just one more slice."

So many of these desserts were served during family gatherings that had nothing to do with holidays or events. They were served simply because someone came over because the day felt long. Because love, in our house, was expressed with something sweet.

I invite you to do the same.

Your Turn to Share

Now that you've explored the flavors and stories of this book, I encourage you to make them your own. Add your own flair. Use local ingredients. Try different shapes or finishes. Make a recipe with your children, with your neighbor, or with someone who needs a little extra sweetness in their day.

Write your own notes in the margins.

Make new memories and new traditions.

Because that's the thing about recipes—they evolve. What starts as a whisper from the past becomes a song in the present. And every time you bake from this book, you're singing that song.

A Tribute to Dziadzia Gienek

I wish you could have met him. He was gentle but sharp, patient but playful. He had a deep, warm laugh and a way of looking at you that made you feel like the most important person in the world. His kitchen was never flashy. It was humble. But it was holy in its own way.

The radio often played softly in the background. There was always tea, always a story, and usually something sweet cooling on the counter. For him, baking wasn't about impressing anyone—it was about *nurturing*. It was about generosity. It was about joy.

That spirit is baked into every page of this book.

I hope when you bake, you feel his presence, just like I do. I hope you feel like you're part of something warm and real because you are.

What Comes Next

Maybe this book sparked a new passion for baking. Maybe it brought back a memory of your grandmother's table. Maybe it simply reminded you to pause and enjoy the process. However this book has spoken to you, I hope it's just the beginning.

Keep baking. Keep sharing. Keep remembering that sometimes the most powerful moments are the simplest ones: a clean fork, an empty plate, a quiet sigh of delight.

Keep creating your own gatherings, whether big or small. Light a candle. Pour the tea. And don't forget dessert.

Thank You

Thank you for allowing me to share my dziadzia's story with you.

Thank you for honoring these recipes with your time and attention.

Thank you for making space in your kitchen—and your life—for the kind of comfort that only a homemade dessert can offer.

Wherever you are, whatever season you're in, may your kitchen be full of light, laughter, and the sweet aromas of tradition.

Until We Bake Again

So here we are—at the end of the book, but hopefully just the beginning of many delicious memories. I hope your heart feels full. I hope your cookie jar is never empty. And I hope, just maybe, this book will become a family treasure for you, as these recipes have been for us.

From my dziadzia's kitchen to yours:

Smacznego.

And don't forget the powdered sugar.

With love and gratitude.

Glossary

Cakes & Tortes (Ciasta i Torty)

1. **Sernik** – Polish cheesecake
2. **Makowiec** – Poppy seed roll
3. **Karpatka** – Cream puff cake
4. **Szarlotka** – Polish apple pie
5. **Metrowiec** – Layered "meter cake"
6. **Ciasto drożdżowe** – Yeast cake
7. **Pischinger** – Wafer cake with chocolate filling
8. **Pleśniak** – Crumbly cake with jam and meringue
9. **Ciasto Stefanka** – Layered honey cake
10. **Tort czekoladowy** – Chocolate cake
11. **Ciasto Izaura** – Chocolate and cheesecake mix
12. **Ciasto jogurtowe** – Yogurt cake
13. **Ciasto zebra** – Zebra-striped cake
14. **Ciasto kokosowe** – Coconut cake
15. **Tort makowy** – Poppy seed torte
16. **Miodownik** – Honey cake
17. **Torcik wedlowski** – Wedel-style chocolate wafer cake
18. **Ciasto z rabarbarem** – Rhubarb cake
19. **Ciasto krówkowe** – Caramel cake
20. **Piernik** – Gingerbread cake

21. **Keks** – Polish fruitcake
22. **Ciasto budyniowe** – Pudding cake
23. **Fale Dunaju** – "Danube waves" layered cake
24. **Ciasto cytrynowe** – Lemon cake
25. **Tort orzechowy** – Walnut torte
26. **Wuzedki** - Chocolate layered cake

Cookies & Small Sweets (Ciastka i Słodycze)

26. **Pączki** – Polish doughnuts
27. **Faworki (Chruściki)** – Angel wings
28. **Kruche ciasteczka** – Butter cookies
29. **Pierniczki** – Gingerbread cookies
30. **Ciasteczka kokosanki** – Coconut macaroons
31. **Ciasteczka serowe** – Cheese cookies
32. **Ciasteczka miodowe** – Honey cookies
33. **Ciasteczka maślane** – Shortbread cookies
34. **Ciasteczka orzechowe** – Nut cookies
35. **Amerykanki** – American-style soft cookies
36. **Ciasteczka migdałowe** – Almond cookies
37. **Ciasteczka z dżemem** – Jam-filled cookies
38. **Makówki** – Poppy seed and milk dessert
39. **Ciasteczka marmurkowe** – Marble cookies
40. **Ciasteczka cytrynowe** – Lemon cookies
41. **Ciasteczka piernikowe** – Spiced cookies
42. **Ciasteczka kakaowe** – Cocoa cookies
43. **Ciasteczka cynamonowe** – Cinnamon cookies
44. **Ciasteczka waniliowe** – Vanilla cookies
45. **Ciasteczka miodowo-orzechowe** – Honey-nut cookies

Pastries & Breads (Wypieki i Pieczywo)

46. **Rogaliki** – Polish crescent rolls

47. **Rogale Marcińskie** – St. Martin's croissants with white poppy seed filling

48. **Kołacz** – Traditional sweet bread

49. **Drożdżówki** – Yeast-based sweet buns

50. **Chałka** – Braided sweet bread

51. **Buchtelki** – Small sweet rolls

52. **Jagodzianki** – Blueberry-filled sweet rolls

53. **Bułeczki z makiem** – Poppy seed buns

54. **Bułeczki cynamonowe** – Cinnamon buns

55. **Kołaczki** – Polish filled pastries

56. **Kiełbasa z makiem** – Poppy seed-stuffed sweet roll

57. **Kukurydziane ciasteczka** – Corn cookies

58. **Marcepanowy rogalik** – Marzipan crescent roll

59. **Babka wielkanocna** – Easter babka

60. **Babka marmurkowa** – Marble babka

61. **Babka cytrynowa** – Lemon babka

62. **Babka czekoladowa** – Chocolate babka

63. **Babka drożdżowa** – Yeast babka

64. **Babka gotowana** – Steamed babka

65. **Babka piaskowa** – Sand cake

66. **Mazurki** – Easter shortcrust pastries with decorative toppings

Other Traditional Polish Desserts

67. **Kogel mogel** – Egg yolk dessert

68. **Kutia** – Wheat, honey, and poppy seed dessert

69. **Ryż z jabłkami** – Rice with apples

70. **Ryż z cynamonem** – Rice pudding with cinnamon

71. **Ryż na mleku** – Rice pudding

72. **Kasza manna na mleku** – Semolina pudding

73. **Zupa owocowa** – Fruit soup

74. **Lody śmietankowe** – Polish-style ice cream

75. **Lody truskawkowe** – Strawberry ice cream

76. **Lody waniliowe** – Vanilla ice cream

77. **Kompot z suszu** – Dried fruit compote

78. **Gofry** – Polish waffles

79. **Ciepłe lody** – "Warm ice cream" (meringue-like dessert)

80. **Krówki** – Polish fudge

81. **Chałwa** – Polish-style halva

82. **Cukierki mleczne** – Milk candies

83. **Śliwki w czekoladzie** – Chocolate-covered plums

84. **Pierniki toruńskie** – Toruń-style gingerbread

85. **Blok czekoladowy** – No-bake chocolate block

86. **Sezamki** – Sesame seed brittle

87. **Krówkowy krem** – Caramel cream spread

88. **Zefiry** – Polish marshmallow-like sweets

89. **Lukrowane orzeszki** – Sugared nuts

90. **Cukierki truflowe** – Truffle candies

91. **Ptasie mleczko** – Marshmallow-like chocolate-covered treat

www.ingramcontent.com/pod-product-compliance
Lightning Source LLC
Chambersburg PA
CBHW082012030526
44119CB00065B/754